WOW
worlds of wonder

installation by Salvador Dalí in Figueres, Spain

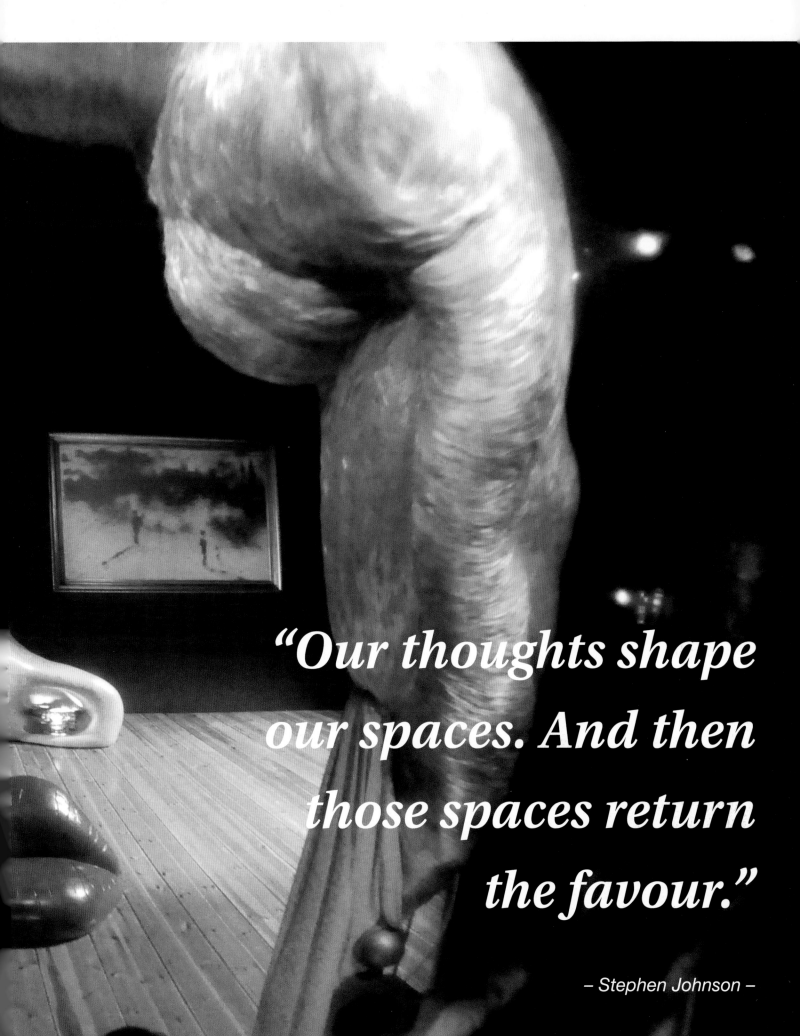

"Our thoughts shape our spaces. And then those spaces return the favour."

– Stephen Johnson –

1 WHAT 2 WHY 3 WOW

3 WOW   4 HOW   5 NOW

INTRODUCTION

This book is about experience design. About creating spaces to inspire people and share stories. This aim, whether pursued by the narrator or the visitor, is as old as humankind. From the caves of Lascaux and the solar temples of Malta to the Museum of the Future in Dubai, it's clear that when humans design a space, they imbue it with a story, and that they have done so since the dawn of time. Some of those places even *embody* human memory. They are full of characters and codes, or use light and space to create certain effects. This happens in the churches of Reims, where edifying parables are depicted on stained glass, on Moscow squares, where bold architecture shows the people who's boss, and in galleries that want to tempt the public to come and marvel at their treasures. It's as present in 18th century English landscaped gardens as it is in contemporary public attractions. You'll find it in theatres, shops, and everywhere else we love going for an experience. The creators of these spaces have learnt how to immerse visitors, using architecture, theatrical techniques, interior design and any other approach that will help create the experience they envisioned.

A BLIND SPOT

If you consider how widespread the practice of using spaces to tell stories truly is and how ineradicable the desire to visit them, it's surprising that *narrative architecture* isn't a first-year course in architecture programmes, or that there's no such thing as *spatial storytelling*. It's true, though: no such field currently exists. The profoundly human tendency to bring people together and immerse them in a joint experience has never been studied systematically.

This book is a modest attempt to do just that. Our company creates Worlds of Wonder, and we've struggled to explain just what we do ever since we first began. It's a curious paradox: we create spaces that tell stories, but it's difficult to tell our own. After more than 25 years of pioneering work, it seemed that the only way was to write our own introduction.

Writing this book has been an exhilarating experience, as it has turned us into students of our own school. Of course, it's not something we're just doing for ourselves. The demons and desires of our clients and peers in the practice of developing experience centres show strong similarities, and if you look at matters in the long run, you'll see that the development of such projects follows relatively fixed patterns. A book chronicling the highlights and pitfalls of this new field seemed like a good idea.

EXPERIENCE DESIGN

Organisations are rapidly becoming more interested in this approach, as many of them are experiencing a growing need to involve their customers in their ambitions and in the world behind the product. They understand that the traditional methods of the past just won't do when it comes to enticing and inspiring their audience. They might have heard someone mention the term experience design at one point or another, but no one *fully* understands what it entails.

Experience Design (XD) doesn't have a very strict definition. If you google it, you'll get bogged down in a mire of definitions, so it's best to steer clear. The concept, however, is extremely popular. 'Experience' is such a common benchmark in the world of design that the term risks becoming meaningless. In all sectors where spaces play an important role, from retail and gastronomy to urban planning, museology, recreation and even natural development and heritage, *experience* is a key term. It might be useful, then, to define what we're talking about.

Of course, this also means we have to consider an immense space that has only emerged relatively recently: cyberspace. In the world of virtual portals, marketplaces, brands and apps, experience is almost more important than in the old-fashioned physical world. The *User Experience*, abbreviated as UX, is the key metric for qualitative design. Although we think that virtual and physical spaces are subject to the same psychological laws when it comes to experience, this book is concerned primarily with the latter. Physical spaces where real people go for real encounters have certain strengths that virtual spaces simply do not (at least, as of now). This book addresses these strengths.

HOW TO READ
THIS BOOK

We will try to find out why now is an especially promising time to set up an experience centre, as well as exploring people's reasons for visiting them. The former will help clarify which requirements these places must meet and the latter will explain how to increase their appeal. We will then use a number of examples to show how you can get Worlds of Wonder to work for you. Finally, we'll describe a number of methods that have proved useful in developing such places. To use a fashionable term, this book is our way of sharing the source code of our profession with anyone looking to get started themselves. The field is so big that it would be small-minded of us to keep the little knowledge we have to ourselves.

This book will cover a collection of topics that might seem incoherent at first, including art, health food, spirituality and the lives of the ancient Romans. We'll talk about leasing cars, roasting coffee and sustainable energy. About nanotechnology, children's hospitals and archaeology. You might not want to know very much about all of these topics. But ultimately, it's about the underlying profession: the ability to turn all these topics into an immersive experience. We're now starting to see the outlines of this profession, and as long as you have a capacity for curiosity, we think you'll find it exciting. When you look closer, coffee beans turn out to contain the same ingredient as a leased car, and you'll find the same ingredient in archaeology and nanotechnology. We'll call it 'interestingness', the mysterious influence that some topics exert on our minds. The fact that this isn't a real word either, says a lot.

THE BOOK IS DIVIDED INTO FOUR PARTS.

Part one defines the most important terms used in this field. On top of that, we investigate the foundations on which it seems to stand. Among other things, we'll give you our personal account, explaining how we found ourselves in this business and what we learned along the way. It is called **WHAT**.

The second part considers the big **WHY** of experience design. We share our vision of what makes it attractive and illustrate this with some case stories and an interview with the man who first identified this field.

The third part, **WOW**, shows different types of application of the World of Wonder approach. We will highlight some examples based on their specific functionality, meaning or impact.

Good news for those with a more practical mind: part four, **HOW**, contains a step-by-step plan for developing an experience centre from the first brainstorming session and initial designs to the financial reports and operation of your very own centre.

Dotted through the book, you'll find *deeplinks* that point you to underlying authors and visions and *cases* that illustrate our thoughts.

NEW LANDMARKS

We think experience centres will play a significant role in the future, one that used to be fulfilled by cafés and the village well, as meeting places where people share stories. These places fulfil a need. More than ever, we see a thirst for communality, meeting people, explanations and understanding, which will help us to make sense of the apparent chaos in which we find ourselves, the changes at hand and the breathtaking challenges we face together.

We think that experience centres will start playing a special role in the future, a function that used to be fulfilled by churches, cafés and the village well, as meeting places where people could share stories.

Within this forcefield, experience centres can become meaning-filled landmarks. They can be the place where organisations explain their intentions, places to discover other people's ideas, or places to fall in love with the world again. That might sound incredibly pompous, especially for a field that, until now, didn't even have a well-defined name. It can be uplifting to remember, however, that it's no less real then when someone in Lascaux decided to paint an ox on a wall. As far as we know, they didn't talk about it too much, but that doesn't make it any less valuable.

Utrecht, the Netherlands, summer 2018

The history of Worlds of Wonder,
the origins of experience design and
the authors' vision on WoW moments.

WHAT

"Everything that is new or uncommon raises a pleasure in the imagination, because it fills the soul with an agreeable surprise, gratifies its curiosity, and gives it an idea of which it was not before possessed."

– Joseph Addison, 1712 –

1.1

WORLDS OF WONDER

what are they and what can they do for you?

Narrative spaces are created by different types of organisations, but their purpose is one and the same: conveying an idea or a story. Because visitors literally walk around in that story, all sorts of subjects can be made accessible. In this chapter, we are going to investigate the architecture of wonderment. In this context, space doesn't only represent the story, but conveys a sense of delight about that story. It's like walking around in the imagination of a curious mind. Hopefully, this will fuel your own curiosity, one of the greatest human faculties. It makes Worlds of Wonder very suitable for strengthening engagement.

BACKGROUND

Worlds of Wonder are used by museums, for example, looking to share complex stories about art, science, or history. Visitors who don't know much about a topic can digest huge amounts of information in one go in these places. A growing number of companies are using this approach to let their visitors experience their brand values. Because all brands want to tell a story nowadays and because these stories simply won't fit into a commercial or internet banner in their entirety, brands create a space where their visitors can experience them in full. These applications have a rich background: religious institutions have been using them for centuries. If you look at a church as a World of Wonder, you'll see what purpose the grand architecture and the stained glass windows serve: they're meant to get you in the mood to internalise a great Story. You'll find an equally ancient example in classical garden architecture, both in the rational or romantic style (the quote on the first page of this chapter dates back to 1712, but it might as well be modern experience design lingo). Both styles say something about the values and vision of the owner. With churches and gardens, it's not about transferring facts but about sharing a mindset. The intention is for the creator and the visitor to meet at a high level of communication. This is a characteristic feature of all Worlds of Wonder.

TERMINOLOGY

In fact, creating a World of Wonder (WoW) is like simulating the world experienced by a curious mind. Looking at it from a more literal perspective, it represents a wonderful environment, or wonder world There are different names for it in different fields. In theatre, the concept of 'narrative space' is used to describe the mindset that the audience shares with the makers. In English, the same concept is also called a *story world*, while the Dutch refer to it as a *beleefwereld*. The Germans sometimes use the word *Raumwelten* (space worlds), in the United States you'll come across an *imaginarium* every now and again and the French use the world *scenographie*. You might also run into an *experium* or hear the phrase *3D storytelling*. In theme parks, these spaces are known as *themed environments* or *immersive spaces*. In the corporate world they're simply called *experience centres* or *experiences*. Museums still use the term *exhibition* to refer to a growing range of narrative spaces. All these words mean approximately the same thing: a space in which visitors undergo a directed experience with a certain content. In this book, we use all terms interchangeably.

EXHIBITION

EXPERIENCE CENTRE

RAUMWELT

THEMED ENVIRONMENT

WORLD OF WONDER

STORY WORLD

NARRATIVE SPACE

EXPERIENCE

WONDER

In a World of Wonder, imagination is king. These places awaken the imaginative faculty of their visitors, which starts to resonate with the story. This is where WoWs distinguish themselves from classical exhibitions and information centres, which are all about conveying facts and teaching their audience. This is not the whole story in a World of Wonder, where the intention is to inspire the audience by encouraging them to engage with a newsworthy story or idea. Wonder is the core part of a World of Wonder, the experience of surprise that makes a strong and lasting impression.

The main underlying idea is that people become more intelligent, more creative and more enthusiastic when they are in awe. Wonder sharpens the senses, encouraging them to feel and taste. It engages the brain to get to the bottom of everything around us and switches on our ability to form a mental picture. On top of all that, it's just a lovely thing. Wonder opens you up to the beauty of the world and lets you give in to new experiences and acquire entirely new ideas.

There is a great need for this. Ideas, inventions, brands, political ideologies, organisations and cultures are all the product of the human mind and they are only useful to the extent that they are also supported and understood by other people. That's where imagination comes into the picture: we might not realise it, but an increasingly large part of our world is becoming virtual. And we're not just talking about bitcoins.

Creating a World of Wonder is like simulating the world experienced by a curious mind.

VIRTUALITY

Take old-fashioned money, for instance, surely one of the more mundane parts of our existence. Money is imaginary. It's made up of coins and paper, or even of bits & bytes. More fundamentally, money is made of agreements. Money works because we share the underlying idea of money collectively. Try using a dollar bill to buy a banana from a baboon. You'll have a hard time fooling the monkey. The dollar bill only has meaning in the human world, because humans collectively believe it has value. This is a great evolutionary advantage. Money makes trading a lot easier, as long as we all believe in it.

The power of collective imagination doesn't only apply to money. Imagine taking the banana from the baboon for safekeeping, promising him that he'll get ten bananas in return when he's in monkey heaven. You will not succeed. The monkey simply doesn't 'do' heaven, no matter how beautifully you may present it. This is very different for people. It has been shown time and time again that people can make even the most demanding sacrifices for no other reason than the promise of some imaginary reward in the future. As far as we can tell, we are the only species that is capable of doing this to such an extent.

The examples of the monkey and our strong collective beliefs were both taken from an historian from Israel named Yuval Noah Harari. In his books, he states that our ability to imagine, the capacity to believe in concepts that we share with each other, is crucial to our success as human beings. After all, there's an immense multitude of concepts between money and religion that we humans have thought up and have actively fostered since: brands, organisations, rules about how we deal with each other, ideas that determine who has authority, values that govern our joint efforts and plans that see us unite behind the promise of a better tomorrow. Our world runs on these concepts, and they're all so obvious that they almost start to seem real. In fact, though, they simply do not exist outside of our collective human imagination.

DEEP
LINK

collective imagination

In his Big History book *Sapiens*, Yuval Noah Harari introduced two concepts that play a crucial role in the success of humankind as a species: the power of fiction and the idea of collective imagination. Not only are these concepts completely ubiquitous in modern society, they are also the perfect way for us to illustrate the impact of imagination.

"Ever since the cognitive revolution, Sapiens have been living in a dual reality.

On the one hand the objective reality of rivers, trees and lions; and on the other hand, the imagined reality of Gods, nations and corporations.

As time went by, the imagined reality became ever more powerful, so that today the very survival of rivers, trees and lions depends on the grace of imagined realities such as the United States and Google."

– Yuval Noah Harari, Sapiens –

It all started about 70,000 years ago, when humankind made a crucial step in its evolution that has proved to be of major importance: we developed the ability to create and believe fiction. Whereas other animal species use communication to describe reality: *"watch out, there's a predator coming!"*, we also use communication to create new realities: *"voting is important for democracy!"*. Shared fiction lets us group together large numbers of people, who can then work towards shared objectives. Our individual qualities did not make us powerful; it's our strength as a group that made the difference. This, in turn, is based on our ability to believe in something together, translating it into coordinated action.

As mentioned in the introduction, we started to deploy this ability in a wide variety of locations and ways. We built pyramids, crowned queens, wrote books and practiced politics, all in the name of a Big Idea. The notion of a Big Idea is attractive, because the world has always been a messy place in which we have had to find our way.

Big Ideas, and the icons of our collective imagination, serve as signposts. And the more they make sense, the more appealing they become. The wonderful thing about fiction is that it has the ability to make you feel part of the bigger whole. People open up more easily to new visions and feel more united. Collective imagination has the amazing capacity to do this on a large scale. That is why epic movies, grand sagas, holy books, Big Ideas and great speeches are all capable of moving mass audiences. They push the boundaries of our daily realities, open them up and create new connections. The same power applies to the monuments, temples, museums and other iconic buildings that mankind has created. These spaces let visitors set aside the realities of life and feel part of an enabling fiction. Creating these spaces, then, is at the core of what we do; worlds where the collective imagination is stimulated in all kinds of ways.

RE-VISION

When ideas are discussed or debated, their self-evident nature vanishes – once we stop agreeing about which future to pursue, for example, or which version of history we identify with. The same happens when ideas become too abstract, too subtle, or too complicated to pick up easily, or when there are simply too many ideas to choose from. When self-evident ideas stop working, it's time to revise them. Time for new ideas, or for renewing our current ideas. In essence, this means we are all faced with a creative challenge.

Create a space for your visitors to engage with the story creatively and attentively: turn it into an adventure.

It doesn't take much to argue that this is the case in our current age. At all levels of our world, ranging from our private lives to the organisations we deal with on a daily basis and the society we live in, values, rules and plans are discussed and questioned every day. The stories we have shared for ages are now being re-evaluated. The time in which we accepted ideas imposed upon us by authorities is squarely behind us. In essence, that's good news, especially when you consider that there's an abundance of creativity in the world and that it's easier than ever to exchange ideas. All we have to do is filter out the right ideas and apply some sense and structure. To do so, we need new tools.

food innovation worlds for *nest*

ATTENTION SPACE

Suppose that you want your organisation to tell a new story, because you think it's relevant to other people. In that case, the situation we sketched above applies to you: you're an institution with a fresh, new idea. It's up to you to ensure that your story is sexy enough to awaken and attract curious minds. To do so, you might create a space for your visitors to engage with the story creatively and attentively: you turn it into an adventure. To that adventure, you add beautiful moments that appeal to all the senses. Finally, you give your visitors the freedom to create their own take on it. If you do that, there'll come a time at which they start sharing their own powerful insights with you.

As said earlier, Worlds of Wonder can be seen as a reconstruction of the mind of a curious person. They not only revolve around providing information, but seek to immerse visitors in a wonderful environment. These visitors don't consume fixed, preconceived stories, but use their experiences in these spaces to create their own. This requires some degree of flexibility on the part of the visitors. Our everyday minds, occupied with our everyday worries, have to be prepared, as it were, to receive big news. Gaining truly new insights, understanding the scope of an idea or the relevance of history, literally requires more attention space.

That sounds a bit like magic, and in a sense it is. All great new insights seem magical at first: hunches that are just as attractive as they are incomprehensible. What might follow is the sudden experience of a broadened perspective. This is what we call a WoW moment, which we'll talk about in greater detail at a later stage. It's only a fleeting moment, but if it's a good one, you'll never be the same again. You'll have gained an insight and be ready to explore it.

STARTING POINTS

Does that mean that it's always a good idea to develop an experience centre? Yes and no. In terms of messaging, there are hardly any topics that *cannot* be turned into a WoW. That's the yes part. But you have to be willing to work for it. Developing and running experience centres can be a demanding task for an organisation. A good story needs an interested listener just as much as it needs a good narrator. This duality underlies the entire development process of a World of Wonder. You'll also find criteria that can help you come to a well-grounded 'No'.

DEVELOP A WOW...

IF YOU WANT TO OPEN UP ABOUT YOURSELF.
Although experience design has a notorious reputation for creating fake worlds, the opposite is true: it turns your organisation into an open house. Just as when you're meeting a real person, openness is a requirement for contact.

IF YOU WANT TO LIVE UP TO YOUR HIGHEST ASPIRATIONS.
A World of Wonder reveals intentions. It involves addressing higher goals, so you must be willing to admit that that's what you're pursuing. Moreover – and this is important – you have to show the world that you're trying to achieve them.

IF YOU WANT TO GENERATE CURIOSITY.
In a World of Wonder, visitors explore the stories and ideas of the hosting organisation. Your organisation must be ready for that.

IF YOU WANT REAL ENCOUNTERS.
People like talking about stories, brands and ideas. There are many ways to do this and experience design can add a new dimension. People often visit experience centres in groups, which means they'll be present in your own facilities, often watching your operations live, and sometimes even interfering with them. Not all organisations are necessarily ready for that.

In terms of content, there are hardly any topics that *cannot* be turned into a WoW.

CONCLUSION

From this point of view, experience centres form a new connection between your organisation and the outside world. They get you real visitors. They make your brand, your history and your plans tangible. All in all, your organisation's objectives will be highlighted like never before. You'll come face to face with your *Why*. It is fascinating to see the number of organisations setting off on this journey of growth. Working with experience centres means thinking about purpose and reflecting on real added value. It reveals that organisations take their Big Idea seriously and genuinely want to build a real bond with their audience.

You'll come face to
face with your WHY.

case nest

The four positive reasons for having a WoW were followed carefully by Nestlé, the world's biggest food provider. Although hit by criticism more than once, the company deliberately chose to develop an open house, showing where it comes from, what it values most and where it is headed.

Nest is built around Henri Nestlé's original factory in Vevey, Switzerland. This is the place where he invented baby milk powder, saving many infants' lives and laying the first foundations for today's huge multinational. Now it's become a welcoming venue where both professionals and families can spend an enjoyable hour or two and get acquainted with the company.

Visitors are welcomed in the open *Piazza*, which serves as a social hub, a relaxing stage for events and a lounge area in one.

In *Fondations*, visitors dive into a series of magic rooms, that describe the origins of the firm. In a fin de siècle atmosphere, Nestlé's first laboratory and an antique factory are presented in a theatrical setting.

Zeitgeist shows 150 years of history through objects, stories and games, addressing some dark pages from the company's history, but also playing with childhood memories.

In *Food Forum*, the company uses engaging interactives to present the global challenges we all face in terms of food & water production. Visitors get a feel for the complexity of these issues and of the struggles involved in doing the right thing.

Visions, the innovation area, is next. Here, Nestlé shows its commitment to food innovation and solving the issue of feeding 9 billion people in 2030. In this spacious pavilion, R&D is turned into playful exhibits.

The boutique and *Café Henri* complete the centre. All in all, *nest* provides an unexpected day out for international visitors, but also a home for all of Nestlé's proud employees.

"The broader one's understanding of the human experience, the better design we will have."

– Steve Jobs –

Jewish Museum in Berlin by architect Daniel Libeskind

1.2
EXPERIENCE DESIGN

a new branch of the creative industry

Worlds of Wonder are designed in a field known as experience design, which produces very different results than other types of design would. Experience design puts visitors in the front seat when it comes to laying out a visitor centre. When it comes to navigation, it even puts them behind the steering wheel. We'll now illustrate this approach and discuss the key components of designing a space based on visitor experience.

WHY A MUSEUM?

Experience design (sometimes abbreviated as XD) is a vast field that can be used for any number of goals, ranging from coding the best software to designing the most hospitable hotel lobby. A key characteristic of experience design is the position of the user or, in our case, the visitor. Why is their experience crucial when creating Worlds of Wonder? Why should we not follow the guidelines set in industrial design or interior architecture, which are a lot more specific? Those fields are also used in designing spaces, so you might ask why we would want to focus on the experience of others.

The added value of experience design is that it activates participation in a remarkable story.

Perhaps we can make matters clearer with the following case. Our agency spent three years working on a national museum about the Second World War in the Netherlands. The generation that experienced the war firsthand will soon no longer be with us. That is why a number of large social funds came up with the idea of creating a museum to keep the memory of the greatest conflict in the history of the world alive. The aim of the museum would not just be to preserve historical wartime collections, but primarily to tell the stories of that time, so that future generations would not fall into the same destructive trap if similar crises and social tensions were to arise again. The idea was to build a museum where the public could step into the shoes of people who had lived through the Second World War. Visitors would find themselves in situations of staged disarray, violence, resistance, betrayal and battle, enabling them to experience what war is like and how they would react in those circumstances. At the same time, they would experience the key historical episodes of the Second World War in a number of chapters.

A large, disused factory was found in the middle of the battlefield of the historic Operation Market Garden. The factory had been built just after the war and strongly resembled an abandoned bunker with enormous dark spaces, large concrete columns and a fantastic view over the river Waal. Here, 48 Americans from the *US Army 504th Infantry Regiment of the 82nd Airborne Brigade* met their demise as they tried to cross the river in canvas boats to free the Netherlands in 1944. Enthusiastically, we started working with a number of museum directors, a historian, a few eyewitnesses and some education experts. Several tens of millions of euros had been made available for the project and three local councils had shown an interest in contributing. In short: this was set to become a project with impact.

One of the major sponsors had selected a rather critical person for the development team. We met every two weeks to work on the concept. Each time, she would ask the same question: *"Why are we creating a museum? Why don't we build a website about the Second World War instead? What kind of information can we not share on a website that we can share in a museum?"* She wanted us to find an answer to that question before her sponsor would pay up.

The museum never made it. As if that wasn't bad enough, the most excruciating part was that she still hadn't understood the added value of a physical museum. Why a museum and not a website? You can publish all the information you could think of in a book, app, or whatever other medium, so it actually wasn't even that bad a question.

The answer is that museums about these subjects don't become relevant until the experience they offer transcends the level of information. With subjects such as these, you need to do more than just provide information. Freedom is an experience that too many younger European generations take for granted. You have to create an *umwelt*, a credible narrative context that tells the audience why the events they are experiencing are relevant. What museums have that websites don't is the ability to immerse visitors in a story. By itself, this is no definitive argument in favour of museums, because a good movie does exactly the same. The key difference between experiential environments and all other media is that visitors are free to move around, make choices and participate actively. In a movie, you follow the fixed perspective of the director, but in a world like this, you are invited to develop your own point of view based on your own experiences. It activates any and all participants. The added value of experience design is that it activates participation in a remarkable story. If we had been able to prove that then and there, there might have been a museum now.

*"I would argue that immersion is primarily
a quality of consciousness that has to do with
the capture & control of attention, a necessary
condition for any interpersonal persuasion,
education or entertainment to occur."*

– Diana Slatterly –

DEEP LINK

barbarism or civilisation?

In 2006, Alessandro Barrico published an influential book about contemporary cultural trends, illustriously titled: *The Barbarians*. In this book, he expressed the unease felt by older generations as a result of the steady decline of old, 19th century ideals, including familiarity with the classics, a love of traditional museums and, more generally, the careful focus required to develop knowledge.

"The profound transformation that has dictated a new notion of experience.

A new location of meaning.
A new form of perception.
A new method of survival.

Not to exaggerate, but I really feel like saying: a new civilisation."

– Alessandro Barrico –

These ideals are threatened by the new wave of barbarism, which has crashed over our culture with a torrent of the spectacular. Over the course of the book, however, Barrico shows that any attempt to protect the past against this new wave is an illusion, and that our entire civilisation is in the midst of a significant mutation. This mutation focuses on a new notion of experience and meaning, the very concepts at the core of XD. Barrico: *"This otherness originates in the realization of what 'experience' can mean nowadays. You might say: meeting the meaning."*

Whereas experiences used to consist of slowly but surely approaching a core meaning, Barrico believes that they are now generated by environments that are easy to enter and exit. Gaining experiences no longer requires meticulous effort, but has become a light, open process that generates energy rather than consuming it.

Meaning has undergone a similar transformation: it has become less absolute, and is rather created by the ability to connect things, to embed new experiences in the familiar. Barrico explains that meaning is not just generated by experiences, but is even multiplied by them. Connecting all our experiences lets us gain greater perspective and understanding.

The rise of experience design is a natural consequence of this mutation: the centrality of the object or marketing objective has made way for a focus on human experience. XD, as described in this book, aims to enhance and enrich us with new meanings. And if people emerge from that process feeling light, open, and energetic, its mission surely has been accomplished.

USERS AND VISITORS FIRST

Experience design is a discipline that takes the end user experience as its starting point. You might think that the end user of products and services is *always* the starting point of all designs, but that isn't the case. A large part of the world around us consists of products and services that were designed with an eye on the production process, not on the end user. That's why some of the objects or services we use in our daily lives are sometimes shockingly inconvenient. Products designed with the end user experience as their starting point are rare, although it's now happening increasingly often. We're seeing more and more companies consider the perspective of the end user, and industrial production processes are being adjusted accordingly.

The *software industry*, the sector that produces the computer programs that we use every day, is a good example. In the past, these programs were designed on the basis of computer logic, which meant that their complexity could drive human beings to utter despair. Programming with an eye on the *user experience*, abbreviated as UX, is now the most common starting point for software development – and we should be very pleased. Using experience as a foundation of product and service design makes them more tangible and understandable to people.

The same happens when designing spaces aimed at communication. *Museums*, for example, love the products they exhibit. Embedding these objects in a history to give them context took second place in the past, and getting visitors interested in these objects took a poor third place. Contemporary museums do the opposite: they determine the visitor experience they hope to generate first, and only then look at how the collections could contribute. As it happens, they have a lot to contribute: nothing makes a more profound impression than real objects. Authenticity is a key factor in experience design.

Companies have also recognised this. Showrooms full of shiny products and slick demonstrations are starting to make way for places where you can experience the idea behind the product, or even the organisation. The authenticity of a company's story plays a major role in this process.

selfie installation at the Heineken experience

experience design (XD) according to Wikipedia

Experience Design (XD) is the practice of designing products, processes, services, events, omnichannel journeys, and environments with a focus placed on the quality of the user experience and culturally relevant solutions.[1] A meta discipline, experience design draws from many other disciplines including cognitive psychology and perceptual psychology, linguistics, cognitive science, architecture and environmental design, haptics, product design, strategic design, information design, information architecture, ethnography, marketing and brand strategy, strategic management and strategy consulting, interaction design, service design, storytelling, agile, lean startup, technical communication, and design thinking.

Experience design is driven by consideration of the moments of engagement, or touchpoints, between people and brands, and the ideas, emotions, and memories that those moments create.

The mission of experience design is to 'persuade, stimulate, inform, envision, entertain and forecast events, influencing meaning and modifying human behavior'.

Experience design is not driven by a single design principle. Instead, it requires a cross-discipline perspective that considers multiple aspects of the brand/business/environment/experience.

While commercial contexts often describe people as *customers*, *consumers* or *users*, non-commercial contexts might use the words *audience*, *visitors* and *participants*.

WIKIPEDIA

AN EXCITING NEW FIELD

Although people are, strictly speaking, also users of exhibition products, we prefer the term *visitor* in these spatial contexts. What we call experience design is linked to this user-oriented approach, crossing many disciplines and having an equal basis in the art of storytelling and theatre. Ancient narrative techniques are typically combined with modern media. It's a whole new endeavour, generating a flock of exciting crossovers. Museums, for example, are turning into playgrounds and festivals now offer places of significance.

We see cool companies equipping their meeting rooms with swings and other attributes that you used to only find in kindergartens, while schools include *serious gaming* in their curricula, which imitates the experience of professional life. Religious communities, such as the Catholic Church, have started using marketing techniques, while brands and celebrities have started adopting the traits of religion. All this makes XD a very exciting field, representing great challenges and new opportunities for the creative industry.

All this makes XD a very exciting field, representing great challenges and new opportunities for the creative industry.

overview theatre at Floriade Expo

XD BUILDING BLOCKS

In summary, our framework for experience design involves directing the visit to a place with the aim of inspiring the visitor with a story or an idea. We don't design visitor experiences; we design the spaces in which these experiences are gained. There are a number of key factors in play, regardless of the subject or the context:

> *"Make your environment a rich one that appeals to all the senses. That does not necessarily mean entertainment."*
>
> *– Dean Krimmel –*

AN INVITATION

People need to know that there's a World of Wonder around and that they're welcome. The invitation represents all parts of the design, ensuring that people feel welcome.

A STORY

The main reason to establish an experience centre is usually a story that is so important that the person who knows or owns it wants to share it with the world. Future visitors might not feel the same straight away. Enticing people to visit an experience centre is an important part of the design.

A PLACE

Although we can't exclude the possibility that virtual spaces will also manage to engage all your senses in the near future, making them attractive destinations, we'll assume for the time being that there's a physical place that can be visited. Places provide context. We call this the *genius loci*: you can feel that you're in a place that has a story to tell.

VISITORS

You have to be able to find people to come to the place and experience what it wants to convey. In experience design, the intended visitors are profiled in advance, allowing the creators to picture their needs as accurately as possible. Mapping these characteristics leads to followers, rather than a target audience: people who come to you because your story interests them.

JOURNEY

You can draw a path between the moment that your followers first get acquainted with what you have to offer, and the moment that they return home, much the wiser. This is often an adventurous journey full of challenges and obstacles. If you look at it from that perspective, being as attractive as possible becomes a game of sorts.

TOUCHPOINTS

In a World of Wonder, visitors come into contact with a story, brand or idea at several moments by looking at objects, playing games or watching a film, for instance. Meeting other people within the framework of the story or performing tasks are also considered touchpoints and stringing these together lets you determine how the story is experienced.

"There is really no secret about our approach. We keep moving forward – opening new doors and doing new things – because we're curious. [...] We call it imagineering – the blending of creative imagination with technical know-how."

– Walt Disney –

1.3
BEGINNERS' MINDS

about the origins of our vision, field and company

In Worlds of Wonder, visitors enter into someone else's realm of thought to gain a fresh new perspective. Tinkering with experience is also known as 'imagineering', a synthesis of 'imagination' and 'engineering'. We will now describe these concepts with reference to our own development, which just happened to lead to the birth of our agency. Education and enterprise both provided building blocks for our vision on experience design.

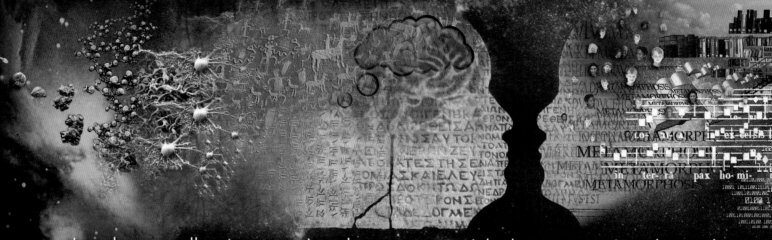

a network of cells in a network of neurosystems in a network of brains

een netwerk van cellen in een netwerk van zenuwstelsels in een netwerk van breiner

interactive wall about network philosophy

ARTIFICIAL INTELLIGENCE

The authors of this book met in 1990, when they were studying Artificial Intelligence (A.I.) at the University of Utrecht in the Netherlands. Artificial Intelligence studies human knowledge processes and models them, so that they can be input into a computer. This lets machines perform complex tasks, such as playing chess, translation and independent car driving. By the time you have your degree, you're a *knowledge engineer*. Breakthroughs in robot technology, facial recognition and automated speech frequently make it to the news: these are all examples of A.I. Machines are starting to show hints of intelligence and it's only a matter of time before there'll be a machine that can keep you company whilst predicting the weather as well. If you use Spotify, or frequently find yourself using Google, you're making use of Artificial Intelligence. This is why these platforms can suggest songs for you to listen to or find the right answers to your questions. Artificial Intelligence, as a field of research, connects psychology with technology. When we started this course, we were both interested in science and humanities. Officially, this field is a mix of psychology, philosophy, computer science, linguistics and neuroscience, and we were taught all of these subjects. For young people with a broad interest, it was one big intellectual playground. In the process, we were given the opportunity to tinker with systems to make them display intelligent behaviour. It's no surprise that the student population was a diverse crew of tech dreamers, part-time philosophers and whiz kids, and the same applied to the lecturers.

Artificial Intelligence, as a field of research, connects psychology with technology.

work of communities in a network of telecommunication is a global mind?

etwerk van gemeenschappen in een netwerk van telecommunicatie is een wereldbrein?

PARALLEL UNIVERSES

Because we were interdisciplinary students visiting monodisciplinary faculties, we gained impressions that you might call superdisciplinary: we saw things that our lecturers did not. It turned out that each faculty was living in its own realm of thought and actively sought to maintain it. The faculties all claimed to operate under the guise of an objective world view –it was scientific, after all– but on closer inspection, it emerged that they all had their own, specific way of looking at the world around them. Remarkably, all these faculties taught us about the same subject: intelligence. Psychologists believed that intelligence was an essentially human feature, whereas computer scientists thought it came down to computing power and algorithms, and linguists tried to find intelligence in the deep structure of language. Apparently, you can interpret the same phenomenon in different ways, even if you're trying to be genuinely objective. The philosophy lecturers added to this confusion by stating that the relationship between human cognitive capacities and external reality has been a subject debated by philosophers for about 2500 years, without any prospect of yielding a result that will appeal to everyone. It's just very difficult to explain precisely how intelligent beings –people, animals or machines– experience reality. Besides, philosophers are annoyingly precise: they love pointing out that you can never be sure that your reality is shared by others. In the meantime, we students tried to seem as intelligent as possible, seeking to understand all these different perspectives.

The various perspectives taken by all these faculties taught us something about how people think in groups. We found that realms of thought really do exist: mental spaces that have their own words, meanings and logical rules. We also saw that multiple domains of thought can exist side by side, like parallel universes. These universes were created by groups of brains thinking together, thus forming a large network. The domains are actively maintained by their members, protecting them from outside influences. This process is primarily unconscious, because all members have a coherent world view that automatically confirms the world view held by their colleagues. Strikingly, this rich insight was given to us by lecturers who were trying to explain something completely different.

Multiple domains of thought can exist side by side, like parallel universes.

A CASTLE IN THE AIR

In 1990, Utrecht University organised an event to celebrate its 350th anniversary, for which we were given the opportunity to present A.I. as a scientific field. Artificial Intelligence would be the theme of one of a number of stands at the event and we were allowed to design and set up one of those. We built a huge computer that people could ask questions about the use and desirability of Artificial Intelligence. The machine wasn't truly intelligent: we were hidden inside the computer to answer the audience's questions, using the giant Windows screen to interact. The trick was to formulate the answers in such a way that people would not be able to determine whether they were communicating with human or machine (in Artificial Intelligence, this is known as the Turing Test). This game of questions and answers navigated the core questions of A.I.: are computers capable of thought? Do they have free will? Can they feel? Typical questions that allow for very learned responses on the one hand and very intuitive answers on the other. We heard both. All sorts of visitors came by to share their ideas, ranging from students and researchers, to visiting uncles and aunts, hospitality staff and security guards. It turned out that everyone was capable of having a good conversation about A.I.

The passionate debate between human and machine turned our computer into a popular attraction. This taught us the lesson about wonder that we shared in the previous chapter: everyone can have a gripping conversation about abstract subjects. What matters is telling the right story. Intellectual capacity, the ability to enjoy thinking about abstract concepts, does not depend on your degree or your IQ. That might not be as obvious as it sounds. In the time of mass media, which has now already come and gone, simplifying messages was the name of the game. Ultimately, this meant that you didn't tap into the creative capacity of your visitors, which is exactly what you have to do if you want them to have new ideas.

People found out about the success of our talking computer, which led to new assignments. We were asked to make a creative contribution to the development of an exhibition about sound and to create a chemistry lab for children. We started our company not because we had ambitious plans for the future, but because we needed a legal entity in order to send our invoices.

FIRMA LUCHTKASTEEL

REALISATIE VAN HERSENSPINSELS

To express the unplanned nature of our business, we called it *Firma Luchtkasteel*. Luchtkasteel is the Dutch word for air castle, a fanciful, unrealistic representation of reality. Our core activity –a mandatory field when registering at the Chamber of Commerce– was 'realising flights of fancy.' A flight of fancy is an unrealistic idea that you might cherish in the back of your mind, but that will usually never become a reality. This is how we were officially listed at the local Chamber of Commerce and in the Yellow Pages.

THE MIRACLE

And then, to our big surprise, more clients started contacting us. Large organisations asked us to consult on questions that they had gotten stuck on, ranging from organisational matters and real estate development to marketing and education, to name but a few. The questions were usually not very strictly defined, and that's why the clients called us. There was simply no one else to tackle them.

We consulted on education policy for a large municipality, came up with an idea for a science centre about the humanities rather than technology and industry, set up a moving caravan for the Dutch Heart Foundation and organised transformational events for the NS, the Dutch railway company. In all these cases, we were told about a problem. It would be up to us to think of a creative solution and start designing all kinds of tools to realise it.

As it happened, our young company, which had nothing to offer but air castles and flights of fancy, met a demand.

Being outsiders, we were able to see solutions that other organisations couldn't. As a result, we didn't just have customers; we had satisfied customers. The open nature of the company functioned as a blank canvas on which others could project their realm of thought. This is when the outlines of imagineering started to appear.

Just as Firma Luchtkasteel was experiencing its first successes, we gained the insight into knowledge domains that we have just shared: the notion that realms of thought arise within groups and are then actively maintained by these groups. Apparently, those realms of thought could be refreshed by introducing new ideas. That was our business: we were outsiders who could provide fresh insights. But what does being *inside* or *outside* really mean? Apparently, there is a boundary between a realm of thought and the area beyond it. The inhabitants of one realm can't see this border, but outsiders can. Besides, it's relatively easy for an outsider to cut holes in the fence, so that creative new ideas can enter.

school classes bringing a robot to life

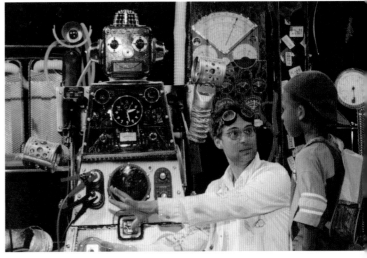

THE FANTASTIC UNKNOWN

This idea turned out to apply to individuals just as much as to groups of people. People create their own realm of thought, which they perceive to be 'the one' reality. New experiences are processed in the context of all previous experiences, Accordingly, your perceived world is shaped, refined and expanded throughout the course of your life. New smells, new political ideas or new tracks on Spotify are all novel in one respect and familiar in another. Spotify uses Artificial Intelligence to carefully assess which track will surprise you just the right amount. Learning is nothing more than fitting new information into your own frame of reference, expanding it slightly.

Just as collective experience, though, individual experience is limited. We might not be able to see our own limits, but they exist nonetheless. This becomes apparent every time that something new catches you by surprise. New tastes, new songs, new people and new ideas constantly demonstrate that there's an endless world to discover. We sometimes call this the Fantastic Unknown. It's unknown because we're not familiar with it yet, and fantastic because realising that you're surrounded by mystery is an exhilarating thought. There's probably an infinite number of things that you don't know.

Taken together, these insights produce a model of perceived worlds of such simplicity that it might almost seem naive. Within the circle, we put all our individual ideas and views: what we know. Outside the circle is everything we don't know: the Fantastic Unknown.

Learning means expanding this circle. Experience design involves playing around with it, deploying any technique that can stretch the limits. Experiences like surprise, discovery, play, suspicion, experimenting, taste, wonder, trying and tinkering all occupy the middle ground between knowing and not knowing.

Challenging people to expand their minds became the *core business* of our agency. Combined with our education in Artificial Intelligence, we saw it as an exciting new challenge, with our company providing us with creative experiments and our degrees proving a source of offbeat ideas. After we left university, neither of us could really define what we really held a degree in. We were now officially knowledge engineers, but in fact we were experts in imagination. Imagination engineers, or imagineers, would be a better fit. Despite this undeniably obscure title and unclear market, we felt that we were sitting on an untapped source of considerable potential. We had enough customers to seriously consider making a living out of it. At the end of the 90s, we took the plunge.

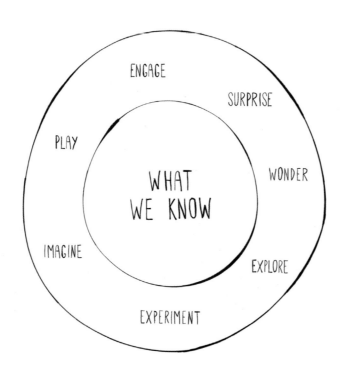

THE FANTASTIC UNKNOWN

ENGAGE

SURPRISE

PLAY

WHAT WE KNOW

WONDER

IMAGINE

EXPLORE

EXPERIMENT

THE TREE OF
KNOWLEDGE
The Biological Roots of Human Understanding
Revised Edition

Humberto R. Maturana, Ph.D
& Francisco J. Varela, Ph.D

biology of creativity

The vision propagated by this book is based on psychology, which has its roots in biology. After all, we're nothing but animals with the capacity for thought.

The biological basis for psychology was laid by, among others, two Chileans in the 80s, called Humberto Maturana and Francisco Varela. They equated psychology with life. A living being, whether an amoeba or a human being, creates a complex relationship with its environment. Maturana and Varela believed that the function of that relationship, the function of life, if you will, is to constantly recreate the relationship. That might sound a bit complicated, and it is. Life, as they see it, is characterised by self-organisation: if something can sustain itself and use materials from its environment for that purpose, it's alive. They call this concept autopoiesis and to this day it's one of the best definitions of life. Self-organisation applies to metabolic processes and all processes resulting from it, including human psychology. According to the authors, our world view has a biological function: it's a way to optimise survival chances in a changing environment. From this perspective, the perceived world we described in the previous chapter isn't static, but subject to constant recreation on the basis of new impressions.

This has three hidden, but incredibly important consequences. First of all, we all have fundamentally different and personal perceived worlds, which we construct privately. We will never share the exact same experience, because we have separate bodies and different histories. The second consequence is that matters are not that extreme. Biologically speaking, all our bodies and lives are rather similar. The third consequence is that we are all permanently creative! Everyone is constantly creating their own perceived world, incorporating all impressions gained from their environment. Because all these impressions come together to form a fairly coherent picture that doesn't change a lot, we might not notice, but it's certainly happening.

These three insights can be very helpful with regard to providing experiences. The first insight teaches you the dangers of a catch-all approach, the second shows that we all have a certain amount of common ground and the third makes clear that your World of Wonder will essentially turn people into creators.

TINKERING

People would often chuckle about our name when we were still called *Firma Luchtkasteel* and Tinker was also met by many with a raised eyebrow. The gypsies who our name referred to didn't always enjoy a stellar reputation. Their work was often considered to be of inferior quality, as opposed to decent craftsmanship. So why the risky choice? Especially if you're trying to rid yourself of your fanciful image, you're just getting started, and you're working in an age that doesn't quite appreciate relativism.

The reason is that we thought it was appropriate to associate ourselves with a somewhat unconventional approach. Besides, tinkering also has more glorious roots: visionary inventors such as Edison and Tesla were called *tinkerers*. Although their approach resembled that of a tinker, they were by no means clumsy or inferior and their pioneering exploits led to numerous innovations.

When you apply the concept of tinkering to the mind, its meaning also changes a little: it approaches the world of daydreaming, of taking visions and seeing whether you can turn them into reality. This felt free and appropriate. By now, history has already caught up with us: there are tinkering studios all over the world, dedicated to visionary tinkercraft. People from a wide range of disciplines have discovered that some solutions are easier to find by simply trying, rather than carefully figuring out every-thing in advance. Our iterative method is still an important part of our approach, which will be explained in detail in part IV.

To top it all off, even we are surprised to see conferences dedicated to making mistakes as a highly efficient way of learning how things should be done! Those gypsies would glow with pride if they knew...

IMAGINEERING

Along with our name, came our subtitle: imagineering. Although we had spent a lot of time thinking of it ourselves, it turned out that the concept had already been introduced by an American aluminium producer in the Second World War. You might not expect it, but they shared our intentions: turning imagination into engineering. It was Walt Disney, however, who made the term famous. Walt regarded it as the core of his business, especially in the 50s, when Disney was still mainly associated with the creation of great visionary projects, such as *Epcot*. In the decades that followed, it became associated with Disney's gift of immersing visitors in a world full of magic, stories and wonder, both on the silver screen and in his ever-expanding theme parks. The main strength is that imagination is king, but that it is engineered to such perfection that the magic becomes a reality. This gift was and still is a source of fantasy for entire generations. In 21st century Europe, imagineering represents a slightly different approach. Psychological impact and social relevance have become more and more important. There is now less emphasis on creating physical worlds, and more on immaterial ways to trigger imagination, as well as an increased focus on inducing positive change and engagement.

"Imagination, the ability to see things which are not yet there, is central in generating new order. [...] Imagineering is a design approach that is oriented towards realising behavioural change by designing a simple positive invitation to make relevance by participating in a collective movement."

– Diane Nijs –

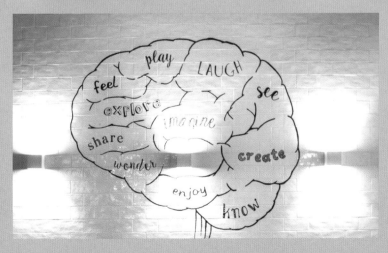

TINKER IMAGINEERS

In 1997, we rented our first office space, and on Monday morning we set off with great excitement, brimming with entrepreneurial desire. We were both in our late twenties. These were the early years of the Internet, so we decided it was time to make a website. We also started looking for a new name, because *Firma Luchtkasteel* sounded too much like a student venture, and 'realising flights of fancy' didn't communicate the legitimacy we were looking for. We did, however, want to remain quirky. We were defined by our fresh approach, the blank canvas, our professional outsidership. We came across the word 'tinker', used to describe gypsies who would wander around cities and villages to do odd jobs that the locals would overlook. They sounded just like the outsiders that we wanted to be. Besides, 'to tinker' turned out to be a verb that meant attempting to repair or improve something casually. The word described us perfectly. Tinker imagineers became our new name and it hasn't changed since.

INSPIRATION COMPANY

Tinker's objective is to stimulate people to expand their perceived world. You could call us an idea agency, but an inspiration company would be more accurate. We focus on stimulating and teasing the limits of perception of individuals and groups. We provoke curiosity rather than transferring knowledge. Our built environments are an intensified version of reality. Wandering about a space like this will automatically pique your curiosity. We then fill this world up with surprises, unexpected twists and turns and inspiring moments. They are Wonderlands that aren't just restricted to Alice. As a result, people are put in the mood to get new ideas and to share them.

We provoke curiosity rather than transferring knowledge.

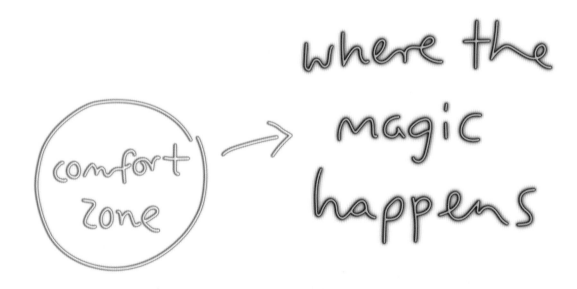

46

TODAY

Speaking of realms of thought: a few years into our life as a real company, the experience economy phenomenon came into vogue, mainly due to the revolutionary book: *The Experience Economy: Work is Theatre & Every Business a Stage* by B. Joseph Pine II and David H. Gilmore, which was published in 1999. This book didn't just give us the language to express what we did as imagineers, but also provided an economic incentive and the beginnings of a market: organisations looking to turn their mission into an experience. We'll speak to the author later on. To our surprise, we found ourselves in the midst of a rapidly growing market, which sprung up around us as if from nowhere. Imagine going for a quiet picnic in a park when you realise, all of a sudden, that you're in the middle of a festival.

Ultimately, we decided to focus on building experience centres with the aim of spreading ideas. Our clients included museums looking to attract new audiences, companies seeking to clarify their mission, governments wanting to strengthen the relationship with their citizens and visionaries attempting to shake up the world. Why these organisations, with radically different backgrounds, were all attracted by spatial communication and why this form of communication is emerging now, in a time where digital spaces are all around us, are two of the questions we'll attempt to answer. The field is in the pioneering phase.

To meet the growing demand and the increasing size of the projects, we were joined by expert creatives: spatial, graphic and audiovisual designers, storytellers and producers who were able turn all these designs into a product. This group of people now works together in an interdisciplinary framework to create experiences for a wide audience. Even in 2018, it's still pioneering work, which we now do with a team of 40. Organisations come to us looking for a new, innovative and honest way to communicate with their audience. We dive headfirst into their field and try to come up with something that hasn't been done before.

We've been doing this for 27 years now, but we're still trying to keep our beginners' minds.

The great thing about this job is that we have a finger on the pulse of the times: sustainability, media technology, healing environments and safety are but a handful of the topics we're currently working on. Nanotechnology, art history, beer, Bali and industrial history are a couple more. Next year, things will be completely different. People sometimes ask us whether it's not exhausting to keep having to learn about new subjects. In fact, it has quite the opposite effect. This work energises us, because it's exciting to discover how people are working on amazing new things everywhere in the world.

Naturally, we're not the only people in the business: experience design has become a real profession. Various agencies have emerged around the world. Every year, technological universities and art academies in particular produce an army of graduates who found new companies that create fantastic new tools: virtual reality, robotics, projection mapping, media installations, blockchain and data visualisation applications are making it from the lab phase to market at lightning pace, which gives us extremely quick access to new resources. In that respect, now is a great time to be an entrepreneur.

All this variety hides a singular, permanent factor that provides a sense of structure: visitors have nothing to do with media technology, architecture or touchpoints. Rather, all they want is to engage with a topic that interests them for an hour or two. If you stay focused on that, complexity can become simple and attractive.

Now we don't just know that *it is possible* to poke holes in someone's world, but we also know *how* to do it. That's what the next chapter is about.

Tinker studio

"Inspiration is what happens when we experience the truth behind the mind."

– John Marshall Roberts –

1.4

THE WOW MOMENT

—

inspiration as a core element of experience design

When you enter a World of Wonder that carries out its task properly, you'll feel an almost physical sensation of awakening and enthusiasm: a WoW moment. These moments can be directed and are the highlight of any visit. All other elements are neatly grouped around it. A WoW moment is meant to entice people to open up to new ideas. That's why WoW moments are perfect in situations where you want to transfer a rich and nuanced story in a short amount of time. This chapter explains how to create these moments and use them to your advantage.

INSPIRATION

We've had a love-hate relationship with the word 'inspiration' ever since we started doing this work. You could regard it as the core quality of what we do, but at the same time it's rather elusive. Simply put, if a space manages to inspire its visitors, we've accomplished our mission. But what does this mean, and can all subjects be inspiring? Is inspiration a supplement to life that some people get to experience and others don't? Or is it the very core of existence: the reason we get out of bed in the morning and go back to sleep at night? Imagine a life without inspiration, or, to stick to the world of business, a brand or story without inspiration. It simply won't resonate.

When our *Handboek voor Hemelbestormers* (*Instructions for Idealists*) came out ten years ago, containing a quirky treatise on the topic of inspiration, the director of an amusement park sent us a critical letter. He appreciated the book, but he thought it was simply wrong that we tried to get to the very nature of inspiration by analysing and examining it. You weren't supposed to think about inspiration, let alone draw up a recipe for it. Nevertheless, here is our second attempt. Inspiration is necessary in the harsh world of news bulletins, overflowing diaries and target audiences looking for meaning. If we can find a definition that can hold up in the everyday world, we might be able to help the amusement park director, as well as all other professional creators of WoW moments.

The etymological source of the word inspiration refers to a breath of air: *spirare* is a Latin verb that means to breathe. When you call someone inspiring, you're saying that they have the ability to breathe life or soul into others. That definition fits in with the diagram we presented in the previous chapter. It's the job of the imagineer to poke holes into someone's perceived world, letting a fresh breeze blow through. This corresponds to our day-to-day experiences: when you're inspired, you feel fresh, happy and cheerful. These moments are usually fleeting but they can be immensely valuable.

It's the job of the imagineer to poke holes into someone's perceived world, letting a fresh breeze blow through.

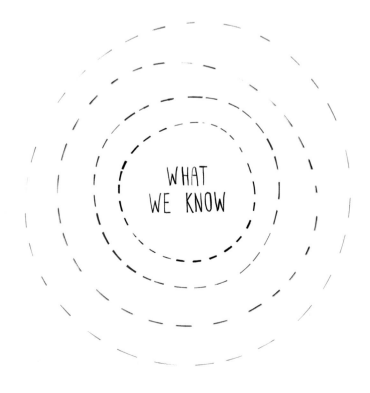

WOW MOMENTS

This experience of expansion is universal. It's the sudden influx of insight, understanding, and joy you experience when you realise the power of an idea. It's also a sensation of great energy when you see something beautiful, or a sense of connection when you meet someone special. A heightened state of perception is a characteristic feature of these experiences: they make you see connections, relationships and meanings that you couldn't see at first, or rather, that you weren't paying attention to. Our day-to-day mind is more focused on making distinctions than it is on seeing connections. When you're inspired, your focus is elevated to a higher plane; you experience the connectedness that underlies oppositions and you gain the ability to discover new layers of meaning. A World of Wonder is aimed at transporting people to that heightened state. This involves all the experiences we've already described, but in this case they don't occur spontaneously. Rather, they're consciously directed.

There's a difference between natural and artificial WoW moments. A lot of enjoyable moments in our lives are experienced in passing. We hardly notice them and we don't typically use them for a higher purpose. A good conversation, a beautiful movie, a sweet gesture: all are part of the natural flow of time and, if all is well, you get to experience them relatively frequently. In Worlds of Wonder these experiences *do* serve a higher purpose: their initiators want you to love the story they're trying to tell. The pleasant sensations that they generate are not meant to bring you into a blissful daze. On the contrary they're intended to wake you up and give you a dazzling experience that you'll remember for a long time to come. We're always looking for a way to produce that spark, caused by the subject in question. If we succeed in doing so, visitors won't just be inspired, they'll be inspired by a specific idea.

THREE SUPER VIRTUES

How can you make a subject inspiring? It's easy to get lost in this question, as we're looking for an answer that applies to *all* subjects, so we can use it as a general framework. Luckily, we can make use of the powerful tool that is ancient philosophy. Plato – whose Theory of Ideas has dominated philosophy for the past 2500 years – formulated three qualities that an idea must have in order to be attractive: it has to appeal to the Beautiful, the True, and the Good. According to Plato these virtues belonged to a higher plane than the human realm of thought, *"spurring us on to do good, to look for true knowledge, and to seek out beauty."*

That sounds pretty good, doesn't it? If we manage to properly express the Beautiful, the True, and the Good aspects of a subject, this apparently encourages appealing ideas.

In principle, you can find the Beautiful, True, and Good in any subject or story. The Beautiful represents the exterior: is it appealing, pretty, or attractive? The True represents the veracity of a story: is it true in all respects? The Good represents the value of a story: what does it mean for us? How does it benefit us? These three qualities can be found in most good ideas and viable stories.

"To make people feel something, you have to not just communicate an idea. You've got to induce the feeling behind the idea. [...] It extends who and what we are."

– Jason Silva –

SOUL

MIND

HEART

BODY

EXPERIENCE LEVELS

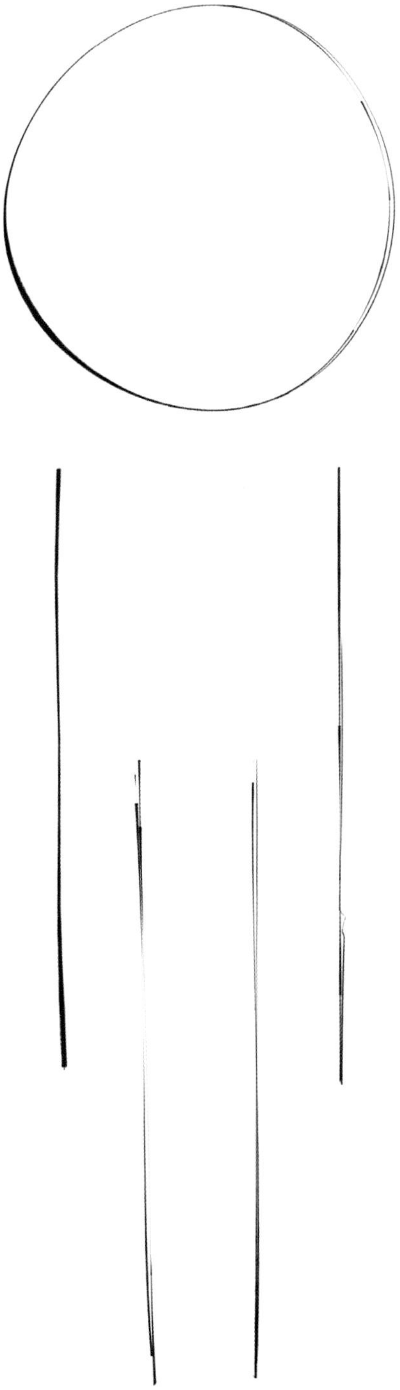

Beautiful, True, and Good may be idea qualities, but how do you transfer these into experiences? Fortunately, we can refer to the four experience levels of humankind: body, mind, heart and soul. This fourfold grouping can be found in cultures all around the world and is easy to verify for yourself. Whereas the body represents sensory perception, the mind consists of our thoughts. The heart is related to our emotions and the Soul stands for a sense of value and purpose.

Inspiration takes place on all of these levels. When inspired, a rush of energy flows through our body, we see things clearly in our mind, a feeling of beauty fills our heart and the soul urges us to do the right thing. Sometimes, you'll feel just one of these sensations, whereas at other times, they all occur simultaneously. Inspiration is created by the free flow of these universal qualities. We open up and experience the world around us more freely. Inspiration is the free perspective. People thrive when inspired and so does the subject of their inspiration; it grows in impact and attractiveness.

Inspiration is the free perspective. People thrive when inspired and so does the subject of their inspiration; it grows in impact and attractiveness.

Simply put, you can see that there really is a general recipe for inspiration: all you have to do is make your space beautiful, interesting, feelable and meaningful.

If a World of Wonder contains these qualities in the right proportion, visitors will be encouraged to engage in the subject. At this point, a WoW moment is within reach.

BODY

The body refers to everything that stimulates the senses. It might be the aesthetics of a building or a beautiful piece of music. This external component comes first in experience design. In a spatial environment this is fairly easy to direct because almost all the senses of the audience can be activated: immersion is the trump card of Worlds of Wonder. As soon as you enter the space, you should be able to perceive the subject. Visitors don't have to understand it immediately, but what they see should get them invested. Essentially you're showing the attraction of the subject.

How can the
subject appeal
to the senses?

MIND

The mind is about the content or the *story*. What is it about? Is it interesting? Am I being challenged? Challenging the mind is crucial because people are critical when they are faced with new information. We live in a world of permanent information overload, which is why most of us are now capable of deciding which information is worthwhile in a matter of seconds. Dwell on an issue too long, and you'll have lost your visitor's attention. The trick is to communicate the story in such a way that it activates people. Preferably, it has multiple layers, so that your visitors can approach it in several ways.

What is
interesting about
the subject?

HEART

The heart makes a story feelable, it knows how to strike the right chord. Exhibitions may look appealing, be very interesting, address a major issue and yet they might still fail to move you. It's often the emotional aspects that hit close to home, redefining your relationship with the subject in question. WoWs are ideally suited for personal encounters. Due to their experiential nature, places are much better at making you feel something than words or images alone. Initiators have an endless range of channels at their disposal to connect with their visitors. It's important to be authentic, and everything that goes along with it. Showing openness and honesty allows for a much better connection than just telling any story.

What moves visitors,
and how can we
make it feelable?

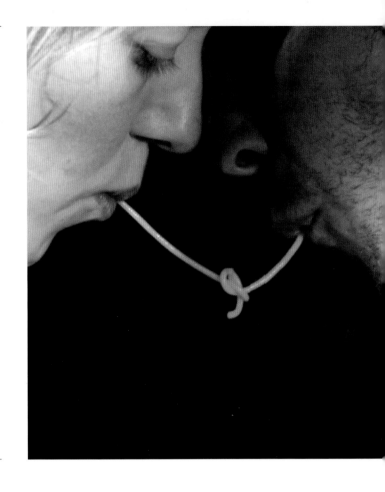

SOUL

Soul finally, relates to the personal relevance of the idea. It should create a sense of purpose and drive people to do the right thing. The question is: do they feel like it is a tool that can help them achieve what they believe is good? The soul originally represented the moral side of the story. In times past, Worlds of Wonder contained all sorts of guidelines for living a good life. Nowadays, we can decide for ourselves what is good and what is not; we've gained a lot of freedom and autonomy. It does not, however, make matters easier, as we all have to find out what is the best life for us. This has led to a great demand for life experiences that give meaning. WoWs contain small pieces of the answer. What matters is that visitors realise that their experiences are part of a larger whole.

Why is this topic meaningful
for both the organisation
and the visitor?

case taste station

A good example of the four levels of experience in practice can be found in a simple food truck that toured the Netherlands for a number of years. It was intended to strengthen the relationship between farmers and consumers. Experience design in its purest form.

The commitment of farmers and commercial gardeners, their passion for their profession and the extremely high quality of their products deserved more attention. That's why their governing federation sent this Taste Station on tour throughout the Netherlands and Germany for several years. The pictures show the bar while it was located in the middle of Amsterdam.

During each tour, the farmers themselves would run the bar to meet urban folk who wouldn't usually come into contact with them. That direct human contact – not with professional hostesses, but with real people with a passion for their product – led to countless real encounters. Heart? Check.

The pictures show a sushi bar rolling past in front of the audience. This bar wasn't filled with fish, however, but with home-grown Dutch delicacies. They had been prepared in a kitchen in the back of the bar and came with a recipe, so that people could also make the dishes at home. The senses were given a real treat, with attractions that delighted both the eye and the tongue. Body? Check.

Finally, the dishes had yet another feature. They all contained a chip that activated a video clip showing a day in the life of a farmer. Lifting the dish and placing it on a plate would play a one-minute video summarising the essence of agricultural work. That's how we catered to the mind.

The real result, however, was the overarching message communicated by the Taste Station: this is Dutch agriculture, it's ours to enjoy and be proud of. Soulful recognition was the lasting effect of this visit, as it revealed a deeper relevance to people's lives.

*"We grow in the light,
but we transform in the dark."*

– Wilbert Alix –

1.5
THE WONDER ZONE

---

the art of balancing magic and comfort

Worlds of Wonder don't just consist of WoW moments. This chapter reveals a hidden force that runs counter to inspiration, but is equally influential. It's hidden because people and organisations don't like showing this side. But if you disregard it, it might end up working against you. If you manage to balance these two forces, you're left with the wonder zone: the playing field for effective experience design.

HARD LESSONS

Inspiration alone isn't enough to win people's hearts. What we're about to describe is very common and very recognisable for anyone who works for a design agency.

A potential client invites us to come up with a proposal for the design and creation of an experience centre. It's a competition, of course, so other agencies will be submitting entries as well. These submissions usually consist of a rough idea of what you want to make, along with a financial proposal.

The subject is interesting, the budget is right and the introductory meeting is going well. There's a click! The clearly defined and inspiring brief includes all sorts of clues about the target audience and the preferred communication strategy.

Right, let's get started! After analysing the subject and identifying the intended visitors, we really go for it in our studio. We get to the heart of the matter, expand it, and come up with an interactive journey with a spectacular finale, of course. Our image wizards transform the idea into a storyboard with fantastic visuals, including animations and audio. We're sure we have this one in the bag, especially after seeing our future client beam with joy as we present our proposal.

They tell us that they're going to phone us in one week to let us know which agency they've chosen, but one week turns into three. On Friday afternoon, we get a phone call and right away it's clear that we're in for bad news:

"I'll just cut to the chase: your proposal didn't make it. It was a very difficult decision, which is why we had to take so long. You stuck close to the briefing and you were our favourite initially. However..."

An ever-different list of reasons now follows, one immortalised in Paul Simon's *50 Ways to Leave Your Lover* (*Just slip out the back, Jack / make a new plan, Stan / Don't need to be coy, Roy / Hop on the bus, Gus, don't need to discuss much...*). How could this happen? Hadn't we mapped everything out meticulously? Were our competitors really that much better? When we went to see the end result a year later, this turns out not to have been the case. A large number of ideals included in the original briefing are nowhere to be found. Did something go wrong halfway through the construction process? Or is something else going on?

We must honestly admit that, in the past, we've been rather upset with clients who, in our eyes, didn't meet their own brief. And we envied our competitors for being more cunning salesmen than we were (that surely was the only difference!). We cried out to the universe, which had us put in so much effort for so little return. It's all just so incredibly unfair!

In reality, things weren't quite that cosmic. Fired up by our enthusiasm, we assumed that the client would simply pick the most inspiring plan. However, there's more than just one mind at the table. They might not have contributed to the *wohltemperierte* briefing, but their voices are clearly heard when it's time to make a decision about big expenses. And here's the learning point: it's not about money. It's about hidden principles that organisations are reluctant to show, but which exist nonetheless.

What goes for our customers also goes for theirs. They too might be puzzled, wondering why they can't get people to visit and might be struggling to make that happen anyway. You can have the world's best location, set up the most exciting offer, have the best possible intentions – and people might still not visit you. Apparently, it's just not enough. There's a counterflow to inspiration, which deserves just as much attention.

some proposals that didn't make it

MAGIC AND COMFORT

You might think that being creative and exciting is always a good thing: the more, the better. This is what is exemplified by the well known idea of magic happening outside the comfort zone (see p. 46). Although true in essence, there's an important limit to it, however. The counterforce to all this is the universal human need for safety and trust. Inspiration is what happens when you manage to stimulate people's imagination just the right amount. If you don't stimulate them enough, they'll remain in their comfort zone, but if you overstimulate them, they'll soon end up in a discomfort zone. This is when inspiration turns into irritation. We have learnt that almost everyone enjoys taking a few steps, but no one likes to take ten steps at a time. That's not surprising, because the term 'comfort zone' is called that for a reason.

It doesn't just pertain to the context of our everyday lives, but also to how we like to see the world. Just think about it: turning everything upside down doesn't sound very pleasant, does it? Slightly stretching your comfort zone feels like a good challenge. But stretch it too much, and you'll just get confused or annoyed. Make something too exciting and it becomes scary; make it too familiar and it becomes boring. The lesson we can learn is that effective inspiration doesn't involve doing everything differently, but experiencing a free version of the familiar. We make the perceived world a little bigger. Things like trust and comfort might not be the first to spring to mind when creating Worlds of Wonder, but they're crucial if they are to be accepted by the target audience.

Inspiration is experiencing a free version of the familiar.

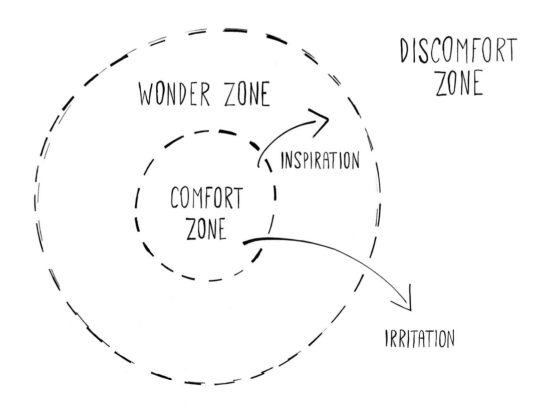

WONDER ZONE

There's a very simple rule to keep in mind: good concepts combine inspiration with guidance. The more innovative your plan, the harder you'll have to work to balance it with comfort. The more exciting your experiences, the more you'll have to focus on bringing the story down to earth. You may choose to lead your experience to a climax step by step, tempting people to join you, but you can also dive in headfirst, reassuring them afterwards by connecting to the world they know. It's important to maintain a balance. This applies to both your relationship with the customer and to well-directed visitor experiences. This reflects the essence of relationships: if you're willing to take care of me, I'll also be more interested in you.

Experience design is not an autonomous art form, where freedom of expression is more important than meaningful communication. Experience design is a means to an end and tries to tell a story. It's only successful if that story is conveyed properly. Art can be shown as it is, as something that is self-contained, or it can be treated as a beautiful topic that may seduce people in countless ways. This allows them to discover and admire both its expression and its meaning, thus connecting comfort and magic. Without inspiration, there's a lot of understanding, but little magic. Without guidance, there's a lot of inspiration, but little comfort. The wonder zone is the area where inspiration and guidance are nicely balanced.

The wonder zone is the area where inspiration
& guidance are nicely balanced.

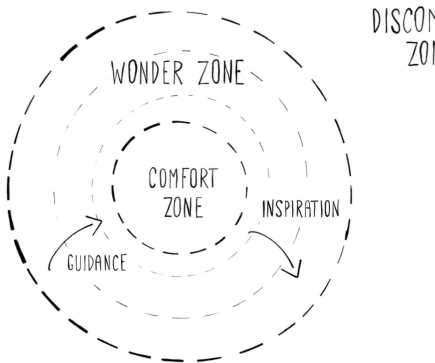

HIGHER STATES AND COMMON GROUND

We can see the movement between comfort and magic as a sequence that brings you to different states. Going from one state to another requires a change in energy and focus. This is influenced by two forces: an inspirational force that draws people to higher states and a guiding force that leads people to more common ground. We experience these states all the time, even when doing ordinary things. Every time we're challenged, we feel the need to relax afterwards. On the other hand when things become too predictable, we go out in search of new adventures. But how do you make this happen effectively? We have found that there are three main communicational approaches when it comes to designing Worlds of Wonder. They all play with the forces of inspiration and guidance in a different way and induce a different state of mind. The art lies in finding a balanced combination of these approaches and knowing how and when to apply each one of them.

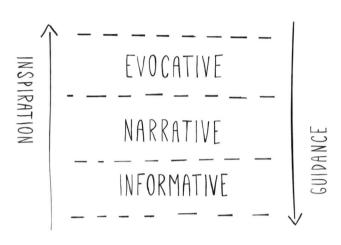

HUMID TROPICS

INFORMATIVE

If you think that your visitors mainly will need guidance, we recommend the informative approach, carefully guiding people's impressions. This mainly consists of conveying your message little by little, appealing to common ground, so that you can slowly introduce them to something new. A calm and factual approach garners trust and understanding, which means people will become more open and receptive. Examples include instructive texts, explanatory stories, infographics and visual overviews. Others are interactive installations, where feedback on people's own actions lets them decide how much further they're willing to go. The feeling of being in control and the link to common knowledge are essential for this approach to succeed.

Information is the ability to guide.

NARRATIVE

The narrative approach is often the backbone of a World of Wonder, because you're trying to convey a story in a coherent way. Storytelling is as old as time, and it's one of the most effective ways to communicate. Expression and meaning naturally go hand in hand. Stories in Worlds of Wonder take all shapes and sizes and are told through various media: texts, audio, audio-visual materials and photographs. Together they should form a bigger picture, connecting separate components to a larger whole. Every good narrative contains suspense, moving people through highlights and moments of rest. The beauty of the narrative approach is that it can effort-lessly transport people from common ground to higher states and back again.

Narration is the
ability to move.

EVOCATIVE

The evocative approach is mainly intended to inspire: evoking an image in the mind's eye. Some means of evocation include Big Ideas, iconic shapes, and surprising creations. All these expressions give rise to a certain mindset that lets you see with fresh eyes: they bring you to a higher state. This can be useful if you want to spark your audience or encourage them to open up. The beauty of the evocative approach is that it allows for personal interpretations that generate inspiration and engagement. It differs from a purely artistic style in that it seeks to evoke a clear sense of meaning, even though it can be understood intuitively. Evocation is often what turns good experiences into Worlds filled with Wonder.

Evocation is the
ability to ignite.

escape helicopter in Ronald McDonald house

UPLIFTING EXPERIENCES

All in all, you could say that we help people to move from one state in the wonder zone to another, sometimes by guiding them step by step and sometimes by enticing them to take a leap of faith. The end result is what you could call an uplifting experience: one that leaves you a bit 'elevated'.

The good thing about the word 'uplifting' is that it implies a positive outcome, but also a balanced approach: people are carefully lifted up from their daily experiences. Whereas creating WoW moments may feel like performing magic, designing uplifting experiences is like applying the art of wonder.

Whereas creating WoW moments may feel like performing magic, designing uplifting experiences is like applying the art of wonder.

"Myths are public dreams.
Dreams are private myths."

– Joseph Campbell –

1.6
EXPERIENTIAL JOURNEYS

—

stages in the
visitor experience

This chapter explores one final aspect of experience design: the time factor. Worlds of Wonder offer a sequence of experiences that are laid out in a specific order. These composed sequences can be considered 'journeys' and there is surprising consistency to be found in their underlying structure. Mapping this structure onto your story can help you achieve the functional goals of your WoW.

TEMPORAL MEDIA

PERSONAL DEVELOPMENT

The previous chapter explained how strong experience centres offer a mix of magical and down-to-earth moments. They offer experiences of varying intensity to convey the Good, True, and Beautiful aspects of an idea. This creates a narrative that is as familiar as it is surprising and as comfortable as it is inspiring. You could compare it to the structure of a good movie: movies that consist only of exciting moments can be unwatchable or, counter to what you may expect, boring. You're also unlikely to finish a movie that's too predictable. A very important stage of movie making takes place in the editing studio, where the recorded moments are sewn together into the most exciting story possible.

Experience centres also tell a story, and in that respect, they resemble movies. The main difference between movies and experience centres is that, in the latter, you are *in* the scene, rather than watching it. Moreover, you can influence the sequence of events by following your own route and expand it through all sorts of activities. To a certain extent, you're an actor in your very own story.

The main similarity is that both are temporal media: time is the key factor in how the story is experienced. Whereas movies use a sequence of scenes, experience centres are based on various interconnected zones and touchpoints in those zones, which are tied together with a narrative. Touchpoints are all the moments at which visitors come into contact with the content. This can be a text, a video clip, an interactive game, or something completely different. Experience centre designers carefully map out these touchpoints, allowing visitors with different preferences to find their own way.

Another similarity between movies and visitor centres is hidden deeper: they both involve protagonists. The structure of all feature films is based on the dramatic development of the main characters in the midst of the turmoil of their mutual touchpoints. In an experience centre, the visitor is that protagonist, whose development mostly consists of internalising an idea. This may sound less dramatic than in the movies, but it's potentially just as intense – or even more so – because it can touch all experience levels: body, mind, heart and soul. Storylines that put this development centre stage often follow a fixed pattern, which has been subject to a great deal of research in film and literature studies. Do stories about personal development share a basic blueprint? Are there any recurring elements? If that's the case, we could use these when designing a narrative space.

Men and women of all ages and cultures are confronted with challenges that they seek to overcome in order to grow.

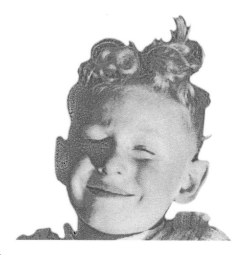

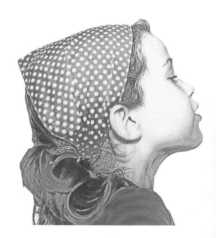

MONOMYTH

CONTEMPORARY MYTHOLOGY

In the previous century, American anthropologist Joseph Campbell studied this type of story extensively. After examining numerous examples from different cultures and different times, Campbell found such a pattern and devoted his life to refining it. He called it the *monomyth*; the primal story of people in transition. He labelled it the Hero's Journey, and many storytellers after him adopted this framework. Greats such as Steven Spielberg, George Lucas and J.K. Rowling all used it to structure their narratives, appealing to a global audience. The fact that it was understood all around the world confirmed that Campbell had hit upon an essentially human process. Each culture brings forth its own stories and its own heroes, but the underlying dynamics aren't culturally determined: they are connected with the human condition. This concept doesn't only relate to fictitious characters, but also to ordinary people in real life. Men and women of all ages and cultures are confronted with challenges that they seek to overcome in order to grow. Campbell called his idea *the hero with a thousand faces*.

Mythology, stripped of its antique, anthropological attire, is about forces that affect a person and that have to be faced when life serves up something unexpected and new. There's nothing antique about that. The Hero's Journey addresses the stages of development that regular mortals go through when they find themselves in a situation that generates substantial new insight, a new skill, or – the ultimate goal – a new way of life. These are exactly the goals modern experience centres strive for.

In a broad sense, the core function of experience centres is the representation of ideas, stories, special places, brands, artistic expressions and inventions – all creations of the human mind. This corresponds to the ideas of Yuval Noah Harari, mentioned earlier. The contents of our collective imagination are partly material and partly fictional. More so, they have a strong symbolic value. The key purpose of experience centres lies in uniting people in a collective understanding of that value. In short: they are about myth.

From this perspective, experience centres are 21st century temples. These temples are no longer inhabited by the gods, but by new ideas. Their visitors are no longer religious believers, they are curious people entering a novel world to gain a new experience. This closely resembles the plot of the monomyth, Joseph Campbell's Hero's Journey. The offerings don't consist of incense or sheep, but of time and attention, two of the most precious commodities of our age. Seen this way, Worlds of Wonder foster growth and transformation.

DEEP LINK hero's journey

The Hero's Journey describes human beings undergoing a personal transformation in various stages. This metaphorical inner journey is represented through a host of culturally defined stories, filled with exciting characters and enchanted adventures. Joseph Campbell identifies three acts: Departure, Initiation and Return, always leading from the known to the unknown and back again.

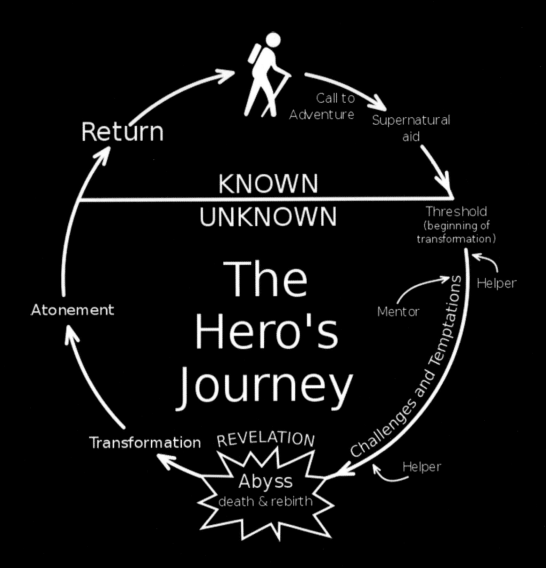

The Hero's Journey

Call to Adventure

Supernatural aid

Return

KNOWN

UNKNOWN

Threshold (beginning of transformation)

Helper

Mentor

Challenges and Temptations

Atonement

Helper

Transformation REVELATION

Abyss
death & rebirth

DEPARTURE
is about the intervention made in the hero's life, which starts with a Call to Adventure. As an ordinary person, they might not feel like going on an adventure (Refusal of the Call) and outside help could be required to convince him or her. This aid can be provided by normal people or take the shape of Supernatural Forces. Ultimately, the hero willingly crosses the Threshold into an Unknown World. This is where the adventure really begins.

INITIATION
is about the hero's subsequent exploits. They face a series of Challenges and Temptations that represent both masculine and feminine powers. The hero manages to conquer all, guided by Helpers and Mentors. All this leads to an ultimate test at the Abyss, where the entire journey will first seem to end in crisis, before making way for Revelation. At this point in the journey, the hero ultimately realises that Atonement (being at one) with the subject of the quest is essential to personal growth, thus generating true Transformation.

RETURN
represents bringing the acquired insights back home. The hero learns how to integrate their adventurous experiences into their day-to-day existence, becoming a Master of Two Worlds, as Campbell called it. Eventually, we come full circle and everything goes back to normal. All is set for the next adventure.

EXPERIENTIAL JOURNEYS

We can use The Hero's Journey to model our Worlds of Wonder by laying out all its steps and mapping them to our narratives. This makes the experience centre exciting and relevant, just what it needs to be attractive. Below, we'll trace the main steps of this journey and look at their implications for spatial design and organisation.

This will hand you a blueprint on which to build your place. Although this doesn't mean that all visitor experiences have the same anatomy, they share a deep underlying structure. The run-up to this visit also has a special role to play, as does returning home. In the section below, we'll go through the successive stages of an experiential journey.

Worlds of Wonder provide a transformational adventure to your visitors, telling an authentic story that's relevant to their lives, using the power of imagination.

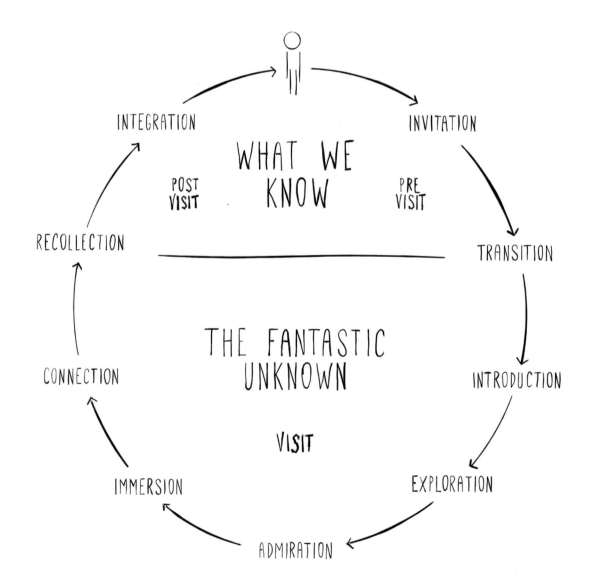

1 **PRE-**VISIT STAGE

INVITATION

Campbell called the first step the *Call to Adventure* and that really is what it should be.

Campbell called the first step the *Call to Adventure* and that really is what it should be. This pre-visit phase is all about inviting, seducing and preparing potential visitors. Given the abundance of opportunities, the need to stand out and to entice people to leave their homes is just as difficult as convincing a Hobbit to embark on a journey to slay dragons. There needs to be a call, which means actively reaching out to people's daily environments, and there needs to be adventure, which means presenting a challenging, yet enticing promise. By starting the journey at home, both means of communication (the invitation and the experience centre) are developed in the same fashion. This is attractive from the start and promises a reward to look forward to.

TRANSITION

A warm welcome
is crucial, since
it enhances both
magic and comfort.

The next step is the visit stage, marked by a transitional area between the normal world and the World of Wonder. In Campbell's journey this marks the turning point, when the main character first sees a glimpse of the adventures to come and leaves their daily routine behind.

In experience centres, visitors are aware that they're about to enter a World of Wonder, so the area is full of promise. A warm welcome is crucial, since it enhances both magic and comfort. Besides the transitional function, this is also the time for practicalities. A range of guidance tools, such as wayfinding, audio guides and floor plans prepares the visitor. These elements are often considered separately from the actual 'experience', but beware: guests will only have one experience – their entire visit! As soon as they pass through the entrance, the core part of the visit has begun.

VISIT STAGE

INTRODUCTION

**Framing a story
properly is crucial
for credibility
and suspense.**

All storytellers know that framing a story properly is crucial for credibility and suspense. This is no different with spatial narratives. In Campbell's mythology, this represents the *Belly of the Whale*, where the hero is immersed in a new environment, not knowing where they are and where to go next. The same sensation might be felt by our distinguished guests, so first of all, they are initiated into the world they've just entered. This is often done by an introductory area featuring evocative elements such as iconic objects, making visitors feel that they've entered a wondrous world. Alternatively, guests are taken on the journey with a more educational approach, such as an introductory video or a personal briefing. People are still happy to follow instructions at this point, because they have yet to understand the context of their new surroundings. In the subsequent exploratory phase, they'll go their own way, at which point it'll be very difficult to group them together and have them listen.

4

EXPLORATION

The key to good exhibition design is conveying a complete context, knowing full well that visitors will not come across all aspects.

Here, visitors encounter all sorts of elements and challenges that playfully enhance their knowledge. This is what Campbell calls the *Road of Trials*. Elements of this stage may include compelling objects, informative videos, interactive games, and anything else you could think of to convey parts of your message. The objects are also called *exhibits*, because they exhibit hidden meaning. The emphasis is on education and engagement. In contrast to the introduction area, visitors are usually encouraged to go their own way. One of the main benefits is that this gets people more actively involved with the subject. This is a crucial element in making sure it's not a mere presentation, but part of a personal journey. The key to good exhibition design is conveying a complete context, knowing full well that visitors will not come across all aspects.

VISIT STAGE

ADMIRATION

Admiration creates a more intimate relationship with the subject.

Although challenges may be very activating, it is important to stay tuned to the promise. In mythology, this part is called the *Meeting with the Goddess*, who shows you how beautiful the world can be, encouraging you to continue on your journey. Moments that evoke admiration do exactly this. Experiencing beauty is truly valuable in itself, but finding new inspiration after all the exploration also makes sure you're still willing to engage. This is the moment to address all the senses and give people an impression of how special, passionate and imaginative a subject can truly be, creating a more intimate relationship with it. This can be designed as a grand vista, an evocative object, a visionary insight or the presentation of a stunning collection. All it has to do is create awe.

VISIT STAGE

6

IMMERSION

The visitor and the subject meet in an intense and intimate way: the story is experienced in an instant.

Many Worlds of Wonder feature one place or moment where visitors are completely absorbed into the story. This part is often theatrical in nature, engaging multiple senses at the same time, which lets the makers control the entire experience. Campbell calls this moment the *Descent into the Innermost Cave*, which is a fitting description of what happens here. The visitor and the subject meet in an intense and intimate way: the story is experienced in an instant. This is often the finale of the visit, but it can also be used to create the right mind-set earlier in the journey. In any case, this is the moment to present a grand vision.

VISIT STAGE

CONNECTION

A strong journey
also features elements
that aim to connect
the story with the visitor
as a person and their
everyday life.

A strong journey also features elements that aim to connect the story with the visitor as a person and their everyday life. Campbell calls this *Atonement*: the moment you realise that this story is about you and that it's time to act on it. Without this step, the experience may be interesting, but not transformational. By creating relevance people realise that the story might have a more personal meaning. This might be considered the big reward that a truly inspiring journey has to offer. This is also key in making sure the insights gathered here are taken home at the end of the visit.

VISIT STAGE

RECOLLECTION

Discussing, classifying and internalising the experience is invaluable, and the more opportunities you give visitors to do so, the more vividly they'll remember their visit.

At the end of the visit there is another transitional area between the World of Wonder and the world of our every-day existence. It's often a shop (exit through the gift shop!) or a café. Both are excellent places for visitors to evaluate their experiences and to consider the takeaway message. The shop does so by offering mementos, with the restaurant giving visitors the chance to reflect and evaluate. Is there any better place to do so than one that was designed with this specific purpose in mind? The word restaurant comes from the Latin *restauro*, which means 'I restore'. Discussing and internalising the experience is invaluable, and the more opportunities you give visitors to do so, the more vividly they'll remember their visit. In some centres, shops and restaurants only feature for commercial ends. Now you know that they can serve a greater purpose.

POST-VISIT STAGE

9

INTEGRATION

The post-visit stage
is about people
converting the experiences
they have gained
into new behaviour.

By now, the visitor has returned from the World of Wonder and they're back at home. The post-visit stage is about people converting the experiences they have gained into new behaviour, integrating the acquired insights into their world view. Campbell calls this the *Master of Two Worlds*, the stage at which the ordinary world and the World of Wonder are brought together. You can help your guests with something called the extended experience. This often involves platforms on social and other media that let people further connect with the subject on a more personal level and translate this connection into actions. In schools, teachers often take time to process everything that has been learned with the entire class.

ADVENTURES

Using this blueprint, we design and test the core elements of an experience centre. Moreover, elements from the wider invitation and evaluation process can be integrated into this framework. Thinking in terms of a journey can help to guide the development process, but the approach described above should never be considered a fixed formula. Using the same template for each experience centre would get monotonous; they'd all start to look the same. Its value lies in the knowledge and appreciation of the impact that each aspect has to offer. This may add another layer of meaning and functionality to your designs. The big difference between designing an exhibition and creating an experiential journey is that in the former the content is king, while in the latter the visitor is the real hero.

Campbell's primal mythology connects the field of experience design with an enormous repository of knowledge about transformative stories and adventures. The movie industry already boasts brilliant examples of how ur-mythology can be translated into a modern form. Principally, we can already copy their genius storytelling techniques and adapt them to a spatial approach. This leads to ever more adventurous experiences that affect visitors ever more profoundly. There's much to be gained if the creators of spatial stories join this movement.

Of course, not all visits to all WoWs lead to radical behavioural changes. Generally, visitors change their attitude towards a subject or story. They're given the chance to engage with and focus on the subject in greater detail by means of the countless media available to them. In that sense, experience centres are very effective: you've spent some time on the actual spot and feel that you've been *initiated* into the subject. That, essentially, is what it's all about. Sometimes, these centres are designed around a so-called takeaway message. The centre's success can be quantified based on the extent to which it manages to change the attitudes of its visitors.

This is important for the economic integration of such a centre, which will be discussed in the next chapter.

transformational adventure, concept visual for the National Geographic Society

2

The reasons why a growing number of organisations are setting up WoWs and the motives for more and more people to visit them.

WHY

"Experiences are as distinct from services as services from goods."

– Joseph Pine –

2.1
DESIGNING FOR THE EXPERIENCE ECONOMY

---

the added value
of experience design

Experience design has the power to support organisations
in expressing their mission. In museums and leisure venues,
it supports the core business of inspiring and educating audiences.
In other organisations, it helps raise the organisation's profile
and can play a valuable role in their public communications.
In this chapter, we will explore these various roles in some
detail, along with the economical added value of WoWs.

DEFINITION

Experience centres aren't just built without rhyme or reason: they must fit into some sort of economic framework and justify their investment. This justification may vary by industry, as the value created by a natural history museum is completely different from the value of a commercial brand venue. Yet they both qualify as experience centres. Whatever their specific context, they all serve an economic function that is about inspiring, educating and influencing their guests. However, the close similarities of the benefits offered by these various experience centres have never been properly explored.

That is, until the publication of The Book back in 1999: Joseph Pine and James Gilmore's *The Experience Economy: Work Is Theatre and Every Business Is a Stage.*

Experience centres must fit into some sort of economic framework and justify their investment.

The authors, two consultants who ran a creative agency in Ohio called Strategic Horizons LLP, sold 300,000 copies of their book, which has been translated into 15 languages. The book was so influential that the experience design industry – which had remained mostly under the radar until then and was considered a niche industry at best – was recognised overnight as an economic force in its own right. Experience, the authors predicted, would become every bit as important an industry as services, product development and retail. In the distant future, they claimed, it would even surpass the economic value of these other industries. Pine and Gilmore's book elevated the concept of experience and made it the new hot topic. It was only a matter of time before some of the major brands and cultural institutions would inevitably co-opt the concept.

THE MARKET

We can divide the market for Worlds of Wonder into a for-profit and a not-for-profit segment. The for-profit segment can be subdivided into consumer brands and business to business. The not-for-profit segment includes cultural institutions such as museums and NGOs and charities. Whereas these markets were once strictly separated, they are gradually coming closer together.

Whereas these markets were once strictly separated, they are gradually coming closer together.

MARKET
FOR-PROFIT

The for-profit segment is growing because of the current trend of companies creating stories around their products. This includes explaining where the product was made, what it's made of and what it was designed to accomplish. For a while, it appeared as though corporate social responsibility and sustainable practices would be passing fads, but now it looks like they're here to stay. Today's businesses use terms like 'raison d'être' and 'social relevance' as part of their everyday vocabulary. We could even argue that the notion of purpose has become critical to their survival. If consumers have a hard time understanding an organisation's purpose, added value or USP, it will not be around for much longer. This has sent many companies on a quest to find the Big Idea that defines them and tools to help them clarify their objectives. Today's experience centres are designed so as to make visitors acutely aware of the brand's mission.

The companies running these experience centres give visitors the opportunity to engage with their brand and discover how their products and processes really work – and, of course, to marvel at their ingenuity. This strengthens the company's relationship with its customers and other stakeholders.

The notion of purpose has become critical to organisations' survival.

MARKET
NOT-FOR-PROFIT

Museums have traditionally embraced Truth and Beauty as their core values - the word 'museum' is derived from the Greek 'mouseion', the temple of the muses. They tend to excel at this, and many experience designers began their careers by creating museum exhibitions. For most museums, the challenge lies not in the quality of their collections or stories – which tend to be top-notch – but rather in marketing their cultural richness and the immense knowledge of their staff to the masses. On top of that, museums deal with the added pressure of having to compete for grants – and that competition is fierce. Grants which used to be awarded as a matter of course are now subject to strict performance requirements. The requirements pertain not just to quality but also to public outreach: how many visitors does the museum attract? Is the experience engaging? Can it attract people who don't usually visit museums?

Museums excel at telling stories, while businesses are experts in selling them.

This is why the aim is to design exhibitions that have the same appeal to visitors as other destinations that they could visit in their free time. It is clear that this approach is successful, as museums all over the world are seeing their visitor numbers rise each year. While they might not necessarily bill themselves as experience centres, museums do stick very closely to approaches adopted by businesses. Vice versa, the new story-based methods employed by businesses see them draw closer to museums. They could certainly learn a lot from each other: museums excel at telling stories, while businesses are experts in selling them.

The third sector to have caught the experience fever is the leisure industry. City centres, theme parks, zoos and nature reserves are now designed with the visitor experience in mind. Shops are transformed into experience stores and entire city centres are redeveloped around certain themes to make them attractive tourist destinations. Leisure businesses could learn from museums, as storytelling is a big part of their identity. Museums, for their part, can look at leisure businesses to learn how to pamper their visitors and make them feel more like highly acclaimed guests.

THE QUALITIES OF EXPERIENCE DESIGN

So what is the real value of experience design? Businesses and institutions now have access to an ever-increasing palette of options to capture and captivate. Yet the same is true for consumers, so despite the extra possibilities, the question of how to reach people remains as complex as ever. We are witnessing a battle for customer attention. Websites, campaigns, participation in trade shows and experience centres are all ways of reaching people. It is the specific qualities of experience centres that can make the difference. Let's take a look at the most important ones.

We are witnessing a battle for customer attention. It is the specific qualities of experience centres that can make the difference.

ATTRACTION

ATTENTION

PRESENCE

ACTIVATION

INSPIRATION

LAYERING

SOCIALISING

ATTRACTION

Experience centres are created by integrating cinematic, theatrical and interaction technologies into a coherent whole. This triggers all sense organs, resulting in magnetising, spectacular shows, expanding your subject to the max.

Integrated experiences engage all the senses.

ATTENTION

You first have to entice people to come to an experience centre, which can be a challenge. But once you get them there, they tend to stay for a while – usually anywhere from an hour to half a day. There are hardly any platforms that manage to hold people's attention as long as that. Visitors will spend several hours focusing on your topic. These places are literally creating an *attention space*. In this day and age, this can be of great value.

There are hardly any platforms that manage to hold people's attention as long as experience centres.

PRESENCE

Many narrative spaces are located in places where people experience *the real thing*: the only surviving prehistoric artefact, the original brewery, the famous library or, when it comes to events, the people with the right mindset. Although you have your smartphone to access virtually all information available anywhere in the world, the *genius loci* remains peerless, maybe precisely *because* all information is everywhere. Worlds of Wonder bring a place to life by presenting the wonders they contain.

Worlds of Wonder bring a place to life by presenting the wonders they contain.

ACTIVATION

In experience centres, people are free to roam around and explore subjects that interest them. Their active involvement lets them engage with the story more intensively than when it's told using other media. The fact that they can be built around a range of activities that let visitors actively control the story enhances their experiences.

Active involvement lets people engage with the story more vividly than if other media are used.

INSPIRATION

Worlds of Wonder offer beautiful, interesting and meaningful stories. The audience is usually not aware of these qualities beforehand, which gives the opportunity to shed new light on matters. When managed right, any topic can be turned into a WoW moment. Of course, some subjects are more suitable for this purpose than others, but tracing the *Why* that underpins any subject always leads to a new source of inspiration.

Tracing the *Why* that underpins any subject always leads to a new source of inspiration.

LAYERING

Experience design tells stories literally from all angles, and often with different layers of meaning. This makes it an excellent way to capture nuance. XD easily lets you highlight different sides of the same story, catering for different levels of expertise.

Experience design tells stories literally from all angles, and often with different layers of meaning.

SOCIALISING

Centres open to the public are much better showcases of your hospitality than any digital portal could ever be. WoWs don't really have visitors: they have *guests*. This is important because hospitality is appreciated by everyone alike. We're social beings, and many of our beliefs are the product of our conversations with others. There are simple ways to make sure people meet each other within the context of your story, which can lead to unforgettable moments.

We're social beings, and many of our beliefs are the product of our conversations with others.

WHAT'S IT WORTH?

Considering all of the above, you'll find that experience centres score highly in terms of impact and intensity compared to other media. The tangible effects of visiting places like these are usually quantified based on the holy trinity of communications: the change in the guest's knowledge, attitude and behaviour with regard to the subject.

These changes can be linked to economic value, which can be measured through surveys or other tools. It would be wonderful if we could accurately predict the costs incurred for and returns generated, but we've been markedly more successful so far at the former than at the latter. But we do have Pine & Gilmore's economic story, which kicked off this chapter. Let's look into it briefly.

The authors sought to understand why people attach so much significance to experiences. First of all, they had to establish that this was actually the case, so they devised the well-known 'coffee value diagram', which charts the value of a kilo of coffee at different stages of the supply chain. When coffee has just been picked, it's only worth about one euro per kilogram. It doesn't really matter where the coffee originates from or who's selling it. In other words, it's a commodity. After being shipped, roasted and packaged, the coffee is turned into a product, worth about 15 euro per kilogram.

By the time the coffee is poured out to patrons in a cafeteria, it's become a service, at a price roughly ten times higher than the product. You could also enjoy the very same cup of coffee on Venice's San Marco Square or in a similarly picturesque destination. Being in one of the most remarkable spots in Europe, now is not the time to start pinching pennies. The coffee has become an experience that costs 10 euros per cup, adding up to more than 800 euros per kilogram. Pine & Gilmore conclude that how a product is perceived, the context created for the product and the experience associated with the product are key to its valuation.

The authors believe this phenomenon does not just apply to coffee or 'theatrical' settings such as tourist squares: they contend that industrialisation will ultimately turn *all* products and services into commodities – and fall prey to price erosion and anonymity. In their own words: *"Overstocked! Undersold. Ten, 20, 30, 40 percent discounts. Half off everything! Buy one, get one free."* This is how the authors describe the downward spiral that all products and services sold in the traditional way will face: the inevitable loss of all margins and distinctions. Ergo: turn your product into an experience and it might earn you a little money. That goes for coffee, but also for travel, jobs, homes, insurance policies, city centres, and degree programmes. The actual value of the product loses almost all significance: what matters is memorability and relevance.

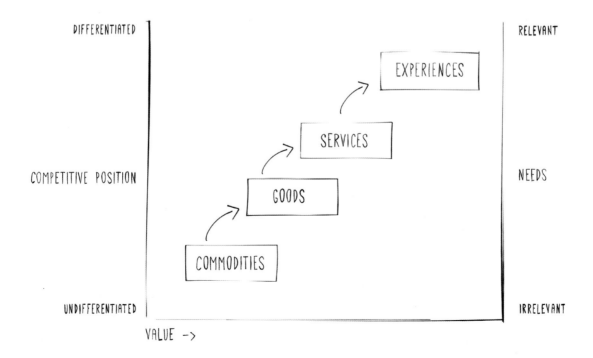

THE NARRATIVE VALUE CHAIN

Will this economic vision apply to the value of stories and ideas as well? Imagine you want to tell a story about the Romans or the Second World War, or that you want to explain the benefits of driving electric cars to a large audience. Can you add value by framing it as an experience? We think you can. Just as with coffee sales, a value ladder can be created for spreading a message, with the original message becoming increasingly 'refined' as it progresses. It starts with a naked fact, a given. If that fact can sell itself, all you have to do is announce it. If, however, it *can't* sell itself, but you still believe it's important that people get to know it, you can embed it in a story. You might compare it to a child who refuses to finish his plate: the problem can be solved once their shrewd carer realises they can transform the fork full of broccoli into an airplane. Packaging facts in attractive context can make them extra exciting or meaningful.

You could even take it to the next level by elevating your story into an idea. This involves turning the story into a creative discovery. You make sure your target audience is moved by the idea, sparking their own creativity. This way of sharing ideas is called 're-creation': a profound means of communication that involves the recipient of the idea creating the idea themselves, as if it were a new discovery. For the person coming up with the idea, it truly is a new discovery, a private WoW moment.

Finally, you can also present your idea as an adventure. The visitor can then fully experience what it means. This helps relate the idea to the person receiving it. In doing so, you can use all the levels of experience: you connect the story to the *body* (by satisfying the senses), to the *mind* (by being interesting), to the *heart* (by initiating a relationship), and to the *soul* (by providing meaning). This value chain can upgrade your facts into relevant experiences.

This value chain can upgrade your facts into relevant experiences.

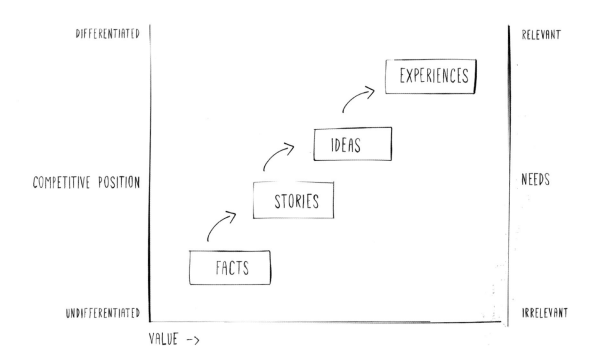

(case) dom under

If you travel to Dom Square in the Dutch city of Utrecht, you'll find a good example of how stories can be layered. By day, you'll see a mysterious portal that grants passage to an underground world, which is actually an exhibition of local archaeological finds. Guests can see the literal traces left behind by centuries of history as they descend into the darkness, ranging from the remnants of ancient Roman roads (the northern limit of the Roman empire,

the Limes, is located just a few metres from this site), to waterworks installed in a rushed attempt to fight a cholera epidemic at the start of the 20th century. These two objects are separated by twenty centuries of religious and urban life. All these centuries-old archaeological finds could be exhibited in a museum, their significance explained through helpful captions.
This represents the *factual* level.

Exhibiting these finds in the exact location where they were found, however and visualising the time layers in which they were found, essentially transforms them. They become protagonists in a *story*. This kind of contextualisation can give objects an exciting, challenging hue – even if they're just a handful of potsherds. Guests use their imagination to glue the pieces together, as they picture how the jugs were used at mediaeval festivals held on the square. All the stories acquired by the visitors are unified within a single narrative spanning 20 centuries of Dutch history, as told by the Dom Square. This storyline has been elevated to an *idea:* this is the oldest part of the Netherlands and you're now in an actual time capsule. As the guests descend

deeper, this idea becomes increasingly credible, a conclusion that they're invited to draw themselves – the recreational aspect. The historians who worked on the excavations developed this insight gradually, and it is now mirrored in the experience of the guests.

To intensify the process, the tour through the cellars was designed to be an adventure: guests are given a torch to explore and the finds are strewn across the soil. When guests highlight objects with their torch, they hear stories through a connected earpiece. This lets each person scavenge the cellars for their own fragments, making them feel like archaeologists on the hunt for important discoveries. Place, objects and stories have been elevated to an *experience*.

THE GOAL SUPREME: TRANSFORMATION

According to Pine & Gilmore, the experiences most valued by people are those that generate lasting changes, and they refer to this phenomenon as a *transformation*. Think back to the most beautiful city you've ever visited, your favourite teacher, or a film that made a lasting impression. They're all moments that will never let go, that changed something within you forever. With the exception of entertainment businesses that specialise in providing escapism, you could state that all providers and visitors are looking for this type of experience. Everyone wants to learn something new: people tend to want to take something away from it. The same goes for the organisations providing the moments: they want them to be as unforgettable and impactful as possible. All of them want to turn their visitors into fans of their story, brand, idea, or solution forever.

Transformations do involve actual change, but that doesn't mean you'll leave every experience centre as a completely different person. Rather, the changes you go through are subtle and specific. However, transformations engage with the very foundations of our needs, the basis of who we are. A transformational experience centre (as far as we know,

there isn't a fixed word for this yet) connects an idea with the origins of who we are. You could compare it to a great movie, one so touching that the audience stays seated while the credits start rolling, simply to digest all that was shown. If you manage to effect a real transformation, you'll have created a permanent connection, one with real, significant consequences.

Evidently, it's about laying bare people's fundamental aspirations and desires. That's nothing new: great communicators know that finding people's deep-seated desires is the basis for all transactions. Apparently, the same goes for experience centres and for any subject that we manage to connect to these desires. We're on a quest for the essential.

To gain a better understanding of this phenomenon, and the growing need for transformation, the following chapter will discuss which motives drive visitors.

"Once the Experience Economy has run its course in the decades to come, the Transformation Economy will take over. Then the basis of success will be in understanding the aspirations of individual customers and businesses and guiding them to fully realise those aspirations."

– Pine & Gilmore –

FROM GOODS TO SERVICE TO EXPERIENCE TO TRANSFORMATIONS

Economical scholars who are occupied with studying experience design report a growing interest in transformational communication. What is a transformation in terms of personal experience and what are the economical consequences? We asked the inventor of the experience economy, B. Joseph Pine II by way of an email dialogue.

From: Stan Boshouwers
Subject: Pressing questions!
To: B. Joseph Pine II

Hi Joe,

As you read in our little bio: our agency stumbled into experience design by tinkering and experimenting in communication projects. Your book gave a boost to the market by specifying 'experience' as a vital economical factor. How did you discover this concept, and what brought you to publishing it? What happened next?

Stan

From: B. Joseph Pine II
Subject: Re: Pressing questions!
To: Stan Boshouwers

Hi Stan,

I discovered the notion of experiences as a distinct economic offering way back in late 1993 or '94 when i was doing a workshop on mass customization. I said something i often did -- that mass customizing a good automatically turns it into a service -- when someone asked, then, into what does it turn a service? I shot back that "mass customization turns a service into an experience!" And went (to myself) "whoa! That sounds good. Let me right that down and figure out what it means...." And so i did, and it meant that experiences were indeed a distinct economic offering, as distinct from services as services were from goods. That meant that there would be an economy based on experiences that would supplant the service economy, just as it supplanted the industrial economy (and the agrarian economy, based on commodities, before that).

Thus was the experience economy born! Well, that's not quite right. Experiences have always been around; they're not a new economic offering, just newly identified. I just put a name to what was naturally happening as economies evolve, and a vocabulary to what great companies like your's were doing to help design and stage engaging experiences.

I even asked the question again -- into what does mass customization turn an experience? That's where i discovered *transformations* -- where companies use experiences as the raw material to guide customers to change, to help them achieve their aspirations. It is the fifth and final economic offering

So i set out to figure out all of the distinctions between each of these five economic offerings, and once i had done that i shared it with my favorite client at the time --Jim Gilmore, then of CSC Consulting. He loved it, so we set out together to figure out what the experience economy was all about, with Jim eventually joining me in Strategic Horizons. We then starting working in earnest on the book, with a publishing contract from Harvard Business School Press. We complete the book in the fall of 1998, just after we published *"welcome to the experience economy"* as a summary in the *Harvard Business Review*. *The Experience Economy* was published in march of 1999, and the rest, as they say, is history.

But really it was just the beginning. When we published the book we talked about "the nascent" experience economy, that we were "shifting into" this new economy. Now -- ever since the publication of our updated edition in 2011 -- we recognize that it is here. We are in the experience economy

Joe

From: Stan Boshouwers
Subject: Re: Pressing questions!
To: B. Joseph Pine II

Hi Joe,

Thanks for your comprehensive reply. It's fascinating to read how you discovered the process, rather than invented it. It bears a striking resemblance to our own history and it is interesting to read that it's what you based your practise on. Probably this way of being perceptive to what is already there, is key to real innovation.

Did the notion of transformation as a fifth and final economic offering present itself immediately, or was it integrated in later versions of the book? We have the feeling that, in Europe, now that everyone has gotten familiar with thinking in terms of experience and the staging of brands, transformation is the next big step. The problem lies with its aura of spiritual enlightenment, while essentially, it is just about offering change to people and organisations how was your vision of transformation received in the us? Do you typically experience cultural obstacles when implementing your vision in other countries? Do you apply a step-by-step method for defining the transformational phases your clients are going through?

From: B. Joseph Pine II
Subject: Re: Pressing questions!
To: Stan Boshouwers

Hi stan

You may be right about discovering, stan! I think it is the right attitude, too, realizing that we all "stand on the shoulders of giants", as Newton said, in discovering what is going on in the universe, and that applies to the world of business.

The idea of going beyond experiences to transformations -- to guiding customers in achieving their aspirations -- actually did occur to me very early in the process of discovering the progression of economic value. I'm always asking "what's next?" And so applied it to the concept of experiences being the next economic offering, so what's next? I realized, first, that experiences could be commoditized just like goods and services. In fact, experiences may be the easiest economic offering to commoditize, for the second time you have an experience it will not be as engaging as the first, the third not as engaging as that -- and soon customers are saying "been there, done that."

Understanding, then, the heuristic that customization is the antidote to commoditization, i realized that it would naturally turn experiences into what we often call "life-transforming experiences" -- experiences that change us in some way. These are transformations, where we seek companies that will help us achieve our aspirations. (I originally, by the way, called these "becomings", but realized that was too "new age" a word for most businesspeople....)

So, yes, this concept of transformations was in the original book, occupying the last two chapters (9 and 10). In fact, in some ways the first eight chapters are just a trojan horse to get people to read the last two chapters! For there is no greater economic value a business can provide than to help someone (consumer or business) achieve his aspirations.

So as you say, Stan, transformation is the next big step, one that people and companies are increasingly ready for. That wasn't always the case, and in the early days i did not talk about it as much. Now i bring it up every chance i get! (Especially when talking with b2b companies, as no business customer ever buys an offering because it wants the offering; its a means to an end. If a company provides the end, rather than the means, it will gain much more economic value.) And people the world over do embrace it much more, both as consumers and as businesspeople seeking to create more value for their customers.

In operationalizing transformations, i always emphasize that transformations are about achieving aspirations, which companies should state in "from/to" statements -- where are customers today (from) and what do they want to become (to). Then they must follow the three phases of transformation: (1) diagnosing this particular customer and his specific aspirations to design the full, customized transformation; (2) staging the set of experiences that will help this person achieve his aspirations; and (3) providing follow-through, ensuring that the transformation takes hold over time.

As the experience economy matures, more and more companies should explore the great opportunities that lie in guiding transformations.

Joe

From: Stan Boshouwers
Subject: Re: Pressing questions!
To: B. Joseph Pine II

Hi Joe,

So, let me get this straight. Experiences are commoditized quickly because if people have had them once, the next time there's the 'been there, done that' posture. Then you say 'customization is the antidote to commoditization' meaning if you tailor your design in a way that generates a unique personal experience, you will achieve the highest attention and appreciation possible, allowing you to touch people in essential ways and thus transforming them. It's like the best book you ever read, the film that opened your eyes, a brief conversation changing you forever. They are the best because they changed you. And that doesn't happen spontaneously, it happens when they give an impulse to your aspirations, to the things you really want to reach. It requires lots of empathy to design this, but it's the holy grail for every organization trying to engage its audience in whatever cosmopolitic issue.

If I understand you correctly, schools, gyms, churches and libraries could be called transformational, since they offer lasting personal growth to people. The thing is, however, that until now it's a 'one transformation fits all' offering, not matching today's needs. If they would succeed in customizing their visitors' experiences, by tailoring their offers to individual clients they really become centres of transformation. One can only imagine what would happen then.

Thank you very much

Stan

From: B. Joseph Pine II
Subject: Re: Pressing questions!
To: Stan Boshouwers

You got it, Stan! As the Experience Economy matures, more and more companies in the industries you cite (and many more) will need to customize guest experiences to guide them in transforming, in meeting their aspirations. Recognize that there is no greater economic value you can provide than in helping people (or companies) achieve their aspirations.

Joe

"Humanism sees life as the gradual process of inner change, from ignorance to spiritual enlightenment through experiences. The highest purpose in life is the full development of your knowledge through a wide array of intellectual, emotional and physical experiences."

– Yuval Noah Harari –

2.2
FACILITATING TRANSFORMATION

the social value of experience design

What makes experience centres attractive? Although online media have now conquered the world and we can consult virtually all databases ever recorded, location-based sources of knowledge and culture are garnering more interest than ever before. In a broad range of sectors, there is a growing demand for thematic spaces that let their visitors engage with topics intensively and deeply. The reasons for the providers of such spaces to do so are clear: it's a great way to tell a story. But what about the other side? Why are visitors drawn to these places? Finding an answer to that question will help when designing them.

A NEW MAP OF HUMAN NEEDS

The previous chapters explained how businesses preferably refer to their highest aspirations when approaching their audience. They show their best intentions and make clear, before all else, that they are driven by an authentic mission. Naturally, they have to make a profit, and there are countless other matters that play a role here, but trends such as sustainability, real added value, and corporate social responsibility seem like they're here to stay. This doesn't just apply to businesses, but to cultural organisations as well. They too must fight for their lives and constantly prove that they are relevant, which is why they emphasise their most relevant and inspirational side. The reverse is also true: that's the side that consumers prefer to see and we might wonder what that says about them. What do we know about people's higher aspirations?

Readers with a background in marketing or humanities know that there's a simple model for this: the elementary pyramid of Abraham Maslow. This pyramid consists of a hierarchy of needs, ranging from basic and material to refined and spiritual. At the bottom of the pyramid, you'll find our physiological needs for food and shelter. Once our needs are satisfied at that level, we automatically proceed to the next level, where you'll find safety needs, or ensuring our continued existence. Ultimately, you reach the top of the pyramid: the level of self-actualisation and other immaterial drives. This pyramid was developed halfway through the last century and was mainly used during that time to decipher consumer behaviour: beneath all our civilised behaviour, we were still permanently on the hunt for material satisfaction. After all, all the lower levels have to be satisfied before we can reach the higher ones.

However, you can also look at this figure the other way around: when there's material prosperity, we all fall upwards.

Once all material needs have been satisfied and taken care of in society, we reach a standard of living that strives for the immaterial. This is a fairly accurate way of describing what's happening in the world today. Shelter, education, health, safety, freedom: for the first time in history, all these needs are within reach for most people in developed countries. These improvements of quality of life can be found all around the world. Although you might not say so after watching the news, simply looking at the statistics shows that it is clearly the case: all these needs, including increasing knowledge, democracy and freedom, are becoming available to more and more people. For the first time in history, more people die of obesity every year than of starvation. This might not be a sign of stellar health, but it does demonstrate growing prosperity. We are moving away from material needs towards immaterial ones, in an upward movement that includes everyone. In rich countries, those ahead of the pack have now made it to the highest level of the pyramid, followed by a huge sprint of breakaway runners.

Following the analogy of a sprint, let's look at sports as an example of this development: 150 years ago, sports were an elite pursuit, because ordinary people spent whatever spare time they had recuperating from their work. Although free time is still scarce, sport has become commonplace. This is a sign of economic progress, because, apparently, we're no longer physically exhausted when we come home.

The same applies to the highest level of Maslow's pyramid. In the recent past, let's say 75 years ago, self-actualisation, in the literal sense of developing your true self, was reserved for people who were wealthy enough to pursue those goals. The rest of the world simply didn't reach that level. Nowadays, most of us are confronted with it, leading to a new set of needs.

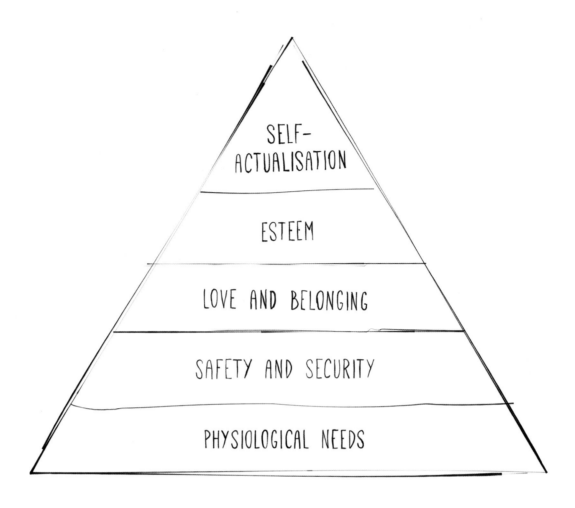

LIFE QUESTS

Maslow said that you just have to look at people's behaviour to find out where they are on the pyramid, where their so-called *life quest* unfolds. This is the dominant mission that people believe they have to fulfil in their lives. Naturally, the other levels of the pyramid also have a part to play in every developed person – you can't really develop yourself when you're famished and shivering in the cold – but the main focus is on the active level, the next step up on the pyramid. You could take our eating habits as an example: most people in developed countries are not worried about *whether* they'll be able to eat, although this used to be our primary challenge for the main part of our history. Nowadays, we're occupied with *how* we eat and what it says about our personality: What do I like? Which food culture appeals to me? How can I stay healthy for as long as possible? Or how could I lose a few pounds? These are today's *life quests*: you are what

you eat. This type of self-actualisation is becoming, or has already become a dominant life quest in many groups in society. Maslow predicted the dominance of this life quest back in the 50s and his successors are already foreseeing new levels (see deeplink: the never ending quest).

A life quest is the dominant mission that people believe they have to fulfil in their lives.

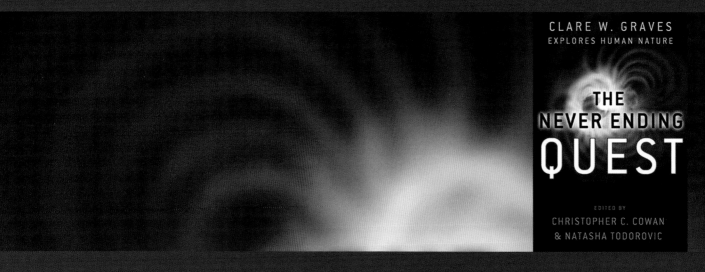

CLARE W. GRAVES
EXPLORES HUMAN NATURE

THE
NEVER ENDING
QUEST

EDITED BY
CHRISTOPHER C. COWAN
& NATASHA TODOROVIC

the never ending quest

The term life quest was coined by one of Maslow's contemporaries in the 50s. This man was called Clare Graves, he wasn't very well-known, and would never climb to fame. He deserves better, because his vision is being used in more and more places all around the world at the highest levels of organisational and community development.

Graves was annoyed by the fragmented nature of his field and decided to combine all psychological models of development known at the time, numbering about 60, including Maslow's model, into a single super model, testing it against his own observations. In doing so, he chose to look at healthy, well-functioning people. This led him to come up with a general model of how people and organisations develop, combining the insights of thinkers spanning two centuries. He called this model the 'emergent-cyclical double-helix model of adult bio-psycho-social development', which might just be part of the reason why he never became famous. Later authors made his vision more accessible

by transforming it into a visual system with easy-to-understand colour coding, known as Spiral Dynamics. Graves's key contribution was the notion that development was an infinite process, which doesn't just stop at self-development, but continues after self-development has been achieved. In the 50s, he predicted a somewhat self-centred phase humanity would be going through (remember the 80s?) and this would be succeeded by a more engaged life quest, focused on finding out how we can take care of our planet together. That achievement is not to be sniffed at, especially if you consider the state of society in the 50s.

SELF-ACTUALISATION

The life quest of self-actualisation involves becoming the most complete version of yourself possible during your life. This applies to many areas, including work, relationships, lifestyle, taste preferences, knowledge, cultural baggage, etc. It doesn't necessarily mean you have to excel in all these areas (although that's how many people interpret their life quest), but it does mean that you have to decide for yourself who and what you will become. You are your own authority. It's hard to imagine now, but for most of our history, we had to listen to other authorities who determined what was True, Beautiful, and Good. Nowadays, we all have to find this out for ourselves. That's a privilege, but it's also a tough task, because it begs the question: How do you do that? Today's ultimate challenge takes this one step further: we aren't just tasked with living our life as we see fit, we also have to determine its purpose. What makes this life worthwhile? Am I spending my time the right way? Am I doing the things that will bring me fulfilment? What is the meaning of my existence and of human existence when I'm gone? To find answers to these questions, people used to be able to turn to the spiritual or political authorities of the community they happened to have been born into. The meaning of a person's life was determined by their church or some other spiritual organisation. Nowadays, you are responsible for finding meaning, within the community in which you were born, or outside it.

CURIOUS PEOPLE

If self-actualisation and finding a purpose are today's life quests, there's a chance that we might have struck upon a challenge faced by large groups of people, including the people you might want to welcome to your centre. Purpose and self-actualisation can sound a little philosophical or even woolly. Most people, however, find their purpose intuitively, by gaining experiences and determining the course of their life accordingly. Take having several life partners before you find the right one, for instance, travelling around the world to meet new cultures, or moving from one employer to another to find a suitable career, and so on. These activities belong to a modern life. Now is the first time in history that we can engage in these activities on a large scale. This might seem like the epitome of luxury, but it isn't really: it's today's life quest.

This might explain why curiosity is so crucial for a successful life nowadays: it's an antenna for new experiences. In terms of our senses, we've become much greater gourmands than earlier generations. In order to carry out our life quest properly, our instruments of perception – body, mind, heart and soul – have become our most important organs, a position that used to belong to our strong arms or quick legs. Nowadays, our sensors are tuned to taste and physical sensations, knowledge, authenticity, sincerity, good ideas, sources of happiness. As such, it's not surprising that a field is emerging that specifically targets those sensors. We develop an interest in authenticity and sincerity, with Beautiful, True and Good experiences acting as our guides.

THE JOY OF CURIOSITY

You might not have expected experience design to be connected to fulfilling our life quest. But just imagine how appealing it would be if there were spaces that had been specially designed for having meaningful experiences. These experiences shouldn't be merely sensational (as in an amusement park), or emotional (as in music temples), nor should they be all about knowledge (as in libraries), or primarily focus on the soul (as in a church): preferably, they should appeal to several of these aspects at the same time. This would give them the chance to become experiences that we can use to calibrate our inner compass. You might have already seen it coming: they're just the ingredients for a good World of Wonder.

Now we might have an answer to the question of why people would want to visit an experience centre. They will do so if it helps them have an experience in one of the countless areas in which they have to find things out for themselves. It's also the first step towards finding out how to make these spaces attractive: appeal to people's curiosity. Historical stories, for example, address the very roots of our identity, which makes them relevant. Plans for the future tell us something about the worlds someone is planning to create, for which they need help. People might want to know what it's like to work for a certain company or how a particular business contributes to society.

They might want to learn new skills or develop their tastes and they might want to broaden their knowledge of how nature, organisations or the entire universe works.

What stands out here, is that an experience centre need not always be usable in a practical way. In that sense, too, we have moved up the ladder. In the past, people would hardly ever learn something new for fun, because they simply didn't have the time. A certain degree of intellectual development was seen as a prerequisite for being a good citizen, rather than as a way to discover the world. Nowadays, everyone has the time and access needed to learn things, and learning for fun has become commonplace. Just look at all the TV channels about science and technology, such as the National Geographic Channel. You'll rarely watch a show on this channel that gives you specific information that you can actually use. Nevertheless, this is commercial TV, and it depends entirely on viewers choosing to watch it. In other words: it meets an actual need. To put it boldly, we might all have become a little bit intellectual: we all search for knowledge every now and again for our own enjoyment. There's an enormous group of people who like doing things out of curiosity. It's not just a pastime: they're actually doing something with their experiences, using all their impressions to build up a world view. This world view ultimately informs their actions.

social engagement: favela painting by Haas & Hahn

UNDERSTANDING YOUR GUESTS

Experience design projects, like all communication projects, define specific target audiences, which model the way we look at people. It can be good to check whether that model does justice to the richness and complexity of the actual people you're inviting. If it doesn't, there's a chance that you're operating with an outdated view of humankind, which means that you will fall short in at least one of the areas of human experience. Don't listen to people who tell you to simplify your message. On the contrary, you should enrich it. Make it attractive to curious minds.

> Don't listen to people who tell you to simplify your message. On the contrary, you should enrich it. Make it attractive to curious minds.

People are complex beings with a great many interests, pursuits, dreams, as well as fears and resistance. They are principally open and fundamentally free. At the same time, they are voluntarily bound by relationships and structures. In general, they're happy with life and the world around them, but sometimes they worry about whether things are headed in the right direction. They know that they are the masters of their own destiny, so they want to experience new and interesting things. These shouldn't be entirely new, but just new enough. In fact, people are just like you! If you zoom out far enough, you'll see that the similarities are greater than the differences. A conclusion that's as intimate as it is public.

Viewed from this perspective, there's nothing wrong with an experience centre that challenges its visitors. You can lure to them to the limits of their comprehension, which, as we mentioned earlier, is where you'll find the wonder zone. You can keep things unresolved or ambiguous, or even reverse them. You can turn your story into theatre and add a touch of magic to your message. Our best projects leave a lot to the imagination, because that's where it all happens. The stories in these projects are open enough that people can't just copy them, whilst still encouraging visitors to tell their friends to visit too. That's what will help your experience centre make a considerably greater impact than what you manage to achieve at the centre itself.

touring caravan and mobile radio station for the Utrecht peace festival

A NEW QUEST

This view of humanity doesn't just let you develop an attractive experience centre for people today, it also lets you fine-tune its mission. Let's zoom out a bit further still, to a view of the entire world. 50 years ago, humankind succeeded in seeing this view for the very first time, when Apollo 14 flew around the moon. The stunned astronauts didn't watch the sun rise, but the earth instead. The photo they took is one of the most frequently shared images of all time. Ever since, astronauts have told us how profoundly moving it is to see the beauty of the world in this way. This experience is known as the Overview Effect, seeing all of humankind as *earthlings*. Accompanying that experience of beauty, astronauts report feeling a sense of vulnerability. We will have to find a way in which we can work together to inhabit and care for the earth as a whole and for each other, as earthlings.

It's highly likely that this, caring for our planet, will be our next life quest. If we don't succeed, we might just tumble down the ladder, at least that is what many scientists claim. If we do succeed, we'll gain access to levels of the pyramid that go beyond our wildest imagination, consisting of a life that's as foreign to us as our modern-day lives are to someone from the 15th century.

What does Maslow's eighth level look like? And what about the 21st? We don't have the faintest clue: all we can see is the current level and the next. Here, the life quest is pretty easy to identify: it's working together on an enormous scale. If that is true, we'll have to significantly improve the way we cooperate.

We believe that Worlds of Wonder can play a significant role in this development and now we know why: they're capable of connecting people at a level that wasn't possible before. By daring to visualise dreams, by making three-dimensional representations of what we have in mind, we can facilitate direct contact between curious minds. We go beyond words and arguments, expressing our wonder in a pure and direct way.

Any relevant topic in today's world will work, because everyone shares the desire to make it more colourful, more exciting, and more vibrant.

In the following section, we'll share some proof of this colourful spectrum.

introductory film ASML experience

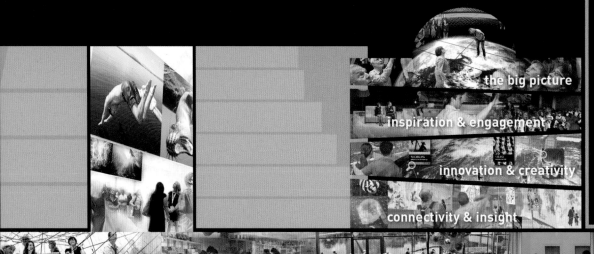

the big picture

inspiration & engagement

innovation & creativity

connectivity & insight

We're building a campus for those who have a passion for adventures, new discoveries and all things real and amazing.

We believe anyone can be an explorer. And all of us can make a difference.

care & curiosity

exploration & discovery

passion & adventure

case

the evolution of curiosity

Everyone knows National Geographic. Some might know the TV channel, others might know it as the 130-year-old magazine framed by the well-known yellow rectangle. You might not know, however, that it's based on a real scientific society, which has its headquarters in Washington D.C.

It's a club of sorts, of which there were quite a few in the 19th century: societies of adventurous people who travelled the world to make discoveries. Most of these associations have disappeared or have been swallowed up by universities over time, but the National Geographic Society is still alive and kicking.

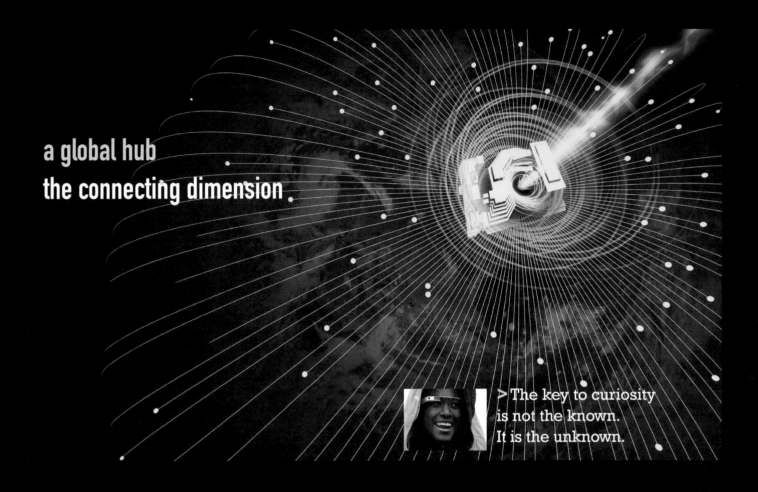

a global hub
the connecting dimension

> The key to curiosity
is not the known.
It is the unknown.

In addition to publishing many magazines and movies, the Society finances research and expeditions. It is and has always been the Society's aim to promote public knowledge and understanding of geography and the world in general. They even do this in their own headquarters, where you can find the National Geographic Museum. By their own standards, this museum was far too static: it didn't do justice to the organisation's adventurous spirit. That is why we explored potential ways in which this museum could be expanded. A dream job for imagineers, especially considering the extremely high quality of the visual world created by this organisation.

The mission of National Geographic is to inspire people to care about the planet and to empower them to make a difference.

That's why we envisioned a transformational experience for its visitors, an exciting opportunity to engage in the brand and to empower themselves. Our canvas was the office building, to be recreated as a campus.

A journey through the National Geographic Campus is like the human journey itself: ascending from our deepest origins, spiralling up above and beyond, driven by an ever-lasting curiosity, a passion for adventure and a quest for the unknown. We envisioned a Maslow-like pyramid of exploration. From the basement to the roof, visitors experience for themselves the many Worlds of Wonder that have been brought to us by National Geographic. And who knows which ones are yet to be discovered?

A hand-picked selection
of WoWs, highlighting their
functions, meaning and impact.

WOW

THE REAL THING
HONOURING AUTHENTICITY

In the middle of Rome's Forum Romanum, an inconspicuous rock lies among all the glorious temples. On the rock, there's a bunch of flowers, placed there by someone in memory of Julius Caesar, in the exact spot where the emperor was assassinated more than 2,000 years ago. That's the power of the real thing. Everyone knows the story of or has seen a movie about the Roman empire, but this is where it all actually happened. That simple fact has so much impact that it's capable of moving people after all this time. People are drawn to this spot in Rome to see it with their own eyes, and to pay tribute.

Despite all the digital realities that experience design has to offer, we must never forget that we're dealing with the real world, full of people, places and objects with wonderful histories.

Seeing them with our own eyes teaches us a lot about our past and also keeps us connected to them. They tell the story of our roots, about how and why we came to be who we are now. Collectively, we marvel at beautiful castles, as the princesses and knights come to life once more in our imagination.

Authenticity is one of the greatest qualities: it involves people, objects and places that exude a sense of place, or that can be made to do so. As for the latter, a helping hand is often required: not to change them into something they are not, but to truly highlight the power of the real thing.

AUGMENTED REALITY 1.0
BRINGING THINGS TO LIFE

Everyone knows them: well-meant exhibitions that, despite their good intentions, simply don't touch you. The real stuff may be king, but that doesn't mean that it is felt, heard, or seen spontaneously. That's why we often treat all those beautiful objects and places as the protagonist in a story that is yet to be told, one that will make you see how special they really are. Generally speaking, this involves setting up a context that causes previously invisible qualities to emerge: Augmented Reality 1.0.

This means bringing to life all those wondrous things that we can't read or appreciate immediately. And there's a great need for that, because many organisations want

to tell their story, showing people why they should come to a certain place or why this particular teaspoon is the most remarkable of its kind. It involves exposing the meaning of what is displayed, restoring its old function in new ways, or imbuing something with a past or a future.

To do so, you don't always have to tell actual stories: highlighting the essence is more important, capturing an idea that viewers can connect with. People are such amazing storytellers that a potent image is often plenty: the audience will supplement the rest with their own imagination. This is how Augmented Reality can come to life in the curious mind.

silver from birth to death

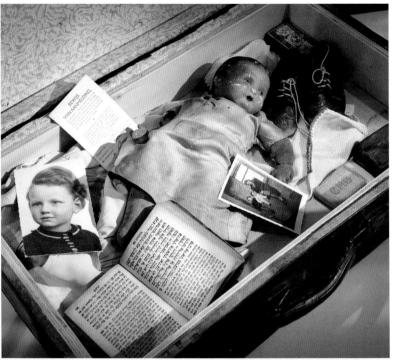

a charred wartime doll comes to life

searchlight reveals the secrets of an Atlantik Wall bunker

UNDER THE HOOD
EXHIBITING INNOVATION

When you take a look inside modern-day businesses, you'll discover a wealth of knowledge, skill and phenomenal performance. The extent and scope of what people make and do is astounding.

Businesses worldwide are significantly ramping up their investments in Research & Development. Take, for example, a dairy company that's identified over 200 different nutritious substances in milk and a food producer that employs 5,000 researchers to look into the future of nutrition. And what about a machine manufacturer that's mastered a chip-etching process with an accuracy of one nanometer? One nanometer. That's how much your nails grow in six seconds.

Clever new insights and smart technologies benefit us, but they're not always equally visible. Even though we now know that milk contains 200 nutritious substances, it still tastes the same, which is a good thing. Processes, products, new ideas and technology exist to serve us, but they're also fun to see and play with.

Open innovation is the magic word. Companies make their source code available to others, so that innovations spread across and beyond the chain. In order to make use of it, you'll have to read the code. Let corporate boasting take centre stage for a change. Make way for the whizzes.

macroscopy of a drop of milk, magnified 100,000 times

seeing through the walls of a smart home

a production chain laid bare

high tech on display

a lab technician speaks with her testing plant behind her

a studio for playing around with mobility issues

ARCHITECTURE, SCENOGRAPHY, MUSEOGRAPHY

CREATING INTEGRATED VISITOR EXPERIENCES

Architecture, scenography & museography are three fields of spatial design that are very different in terms of scope, style and expertise. Since visitors only have a single experience, though, it might be a good idea to synchronise their impact.

Architecture revolves around creating or restoring the built context within which a particular experience is set to take place. There's plenty of architecture out there that's mainly self-contained. The main objective is often to create a building that will last for 100 years and has only a tenuous relationship with its public function. This is a missed opportunity. Nobody will buy a ticket for a building alone: it's what happens inside that matters to visitors. That's why the best projects are those where architecture and experience design reinforce each other.

Scenography is about designing the narrative space of the building in question. Designing, here, doesn't pertain to picking the best tables or deciding on what colour the carpet should be, but to creating a spatial experience, connected to a story. Key questions are: what can I feel, what's the ambiance like, what does this space express?

Some professionals associate this approach with old-school set design. But contemporary scenography has learnt a great deal from the world of theatre, which means that interpretation is now much more important than reconstruction. Creating a mindset rather than a movie set.

Originally, museography represents the expertise of designing an exhibition. Where scenography evokes the feeling of being inside a narrative environment, museography creates carefully designed spaces where visitors are generally aware of the artificiality of their surroundings. It sees visitors mainly as spectators and users and its focus is mainly on the aesthetic, practical and communicational aspects of design.

Although all three fields constitute different approaches to design, they can equally be seen as subsequent layers in a complete experience design package. The role of architecture is to provide an enticing home and context for the entire experience. Scenography lets the visitors embark on an experiential journey and museography designs the touchpoints along the way. Such an integrated approach creates experiences with maximum impact.

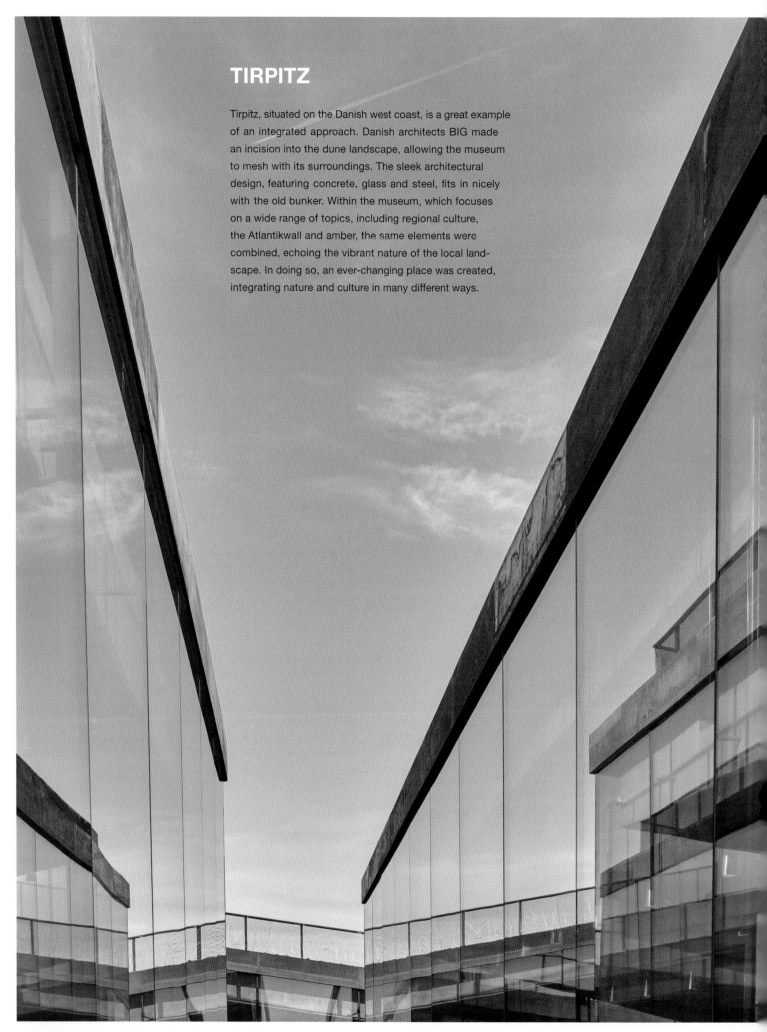

TIRPITZ

Tirpitz, situated on the Danish west coast, is a great example of an integrated approach. Danish architects BIG made an incision into the dune landscape, allowing the museum to mesh with its surroundings. The sleek architectural design, featuring concrete, glass and steel, fits in nicely with the old bunker. Within the museum, which focuses on a wide range of topics, including regional culture, the Atlantikwall and amber, the same elements were combined, echoing the vibrant nature of the local landscape. In doing so, an ever-changing place was created, integrating nature and culture in many different ways.

1ST PERSON PERSPECTIVE
ENHANCING EMOTIONAL IMPACT

After watching the first twenty minutes of Steven Spielberg's 'Saving Private Ryan', you'll never think about D-Day the same way again. In the opening scene, the director transports the viewers to Omaha Beach on 6 June 1944, showcasing the strength of the 1st person perspective. The scene was shot as if through the eyes of a soldier: in the moment, unfiltered, direct. You feel the chaos and fear as if you were actually there yourself.

This almost impressionistic approach also works well for art projects, where the goal is to get personal passion and creativity across. Vincent's vision or Mondriaan's thinking can be seen, heard and felt.

This leads to a more evocative understanding. The 1st person perspective is particularly well-suited for emotional experiences, such as the ones that involve fears, joys or flashes of insight. Creating a subjective reality in the design allows you to enhance this personal perspective. By projecting the emotions involved –scared, tired, excited, amazed– and the associated perceptions onto the visitors' surroundings, you can make them experience that same intimate feeling. This makes WoW moments even more intense.

scene from Saving Private Ryan

1st person perspective in the Airborne Experience

1940 bombing of Rotterdam

seeing through Van Gogh's eyes

Mondriaan's creation of the Victory Boogie Woogie interpreted

A CASE FOR CURIOSITY
QUESTIONS AS ENGAGEMENT DRIVERS

Questions are among the most potent scientific tools. A well-formulated question directs research projects and organises the collective curiosity of learned minds. You might even say that questions are the ultimate driving force. When all questions have been answered, science will be over. We can only hope and expect that it will never actually come to this.

So, questions it is.

And what do the world's science centres have to offer, the places where science is brought to the attention of the general public?

Everything we *know*: facts and history. And do-it-yourself tests that come with pre-written answers. *To do and notice*, as if wonder is something that should be avoided at all costs. It's all well-intended: when you explain everything, everyone understands what you're talking about. There's a high price to pay though: curious minds are not stimulated in this manner. And that was the very reason for opening the science centre in the first place.

It's not difficult to do something about this. Everyone is curious: it's in our DNA. When scientists start sharing the source of their fascination rather than their satisfaction, we'll end up with sparkling exhibitions. In this case: 500 years of curiosity, depicted in an anatomical theatre, with the cosmology of the time projected on the ceiling.

RELIGION FOR ATHEISTS
NEW PLACES FOR THE SPIRIT

In many countries throughout the world, churches are emptying because more and more people have stopped following authoritarian religions. However, we all still struggle with life and sometimes need places where we can sit down and come back to our senses. Where are these spaces to think, reflect on your sins or rediscover your spirit?

There might be a need for new places where we can examine our lives in the most profound manner. No authorities will be worshipped in those centres,

however: now we'll consult ourselves. If you gather the courage to do so communally, you'll experience that we all suffer from the same things and that life's challenges have essentially been the same for centuries. Whatever our contemporary life quests will be, some things are a struggle for eternity.

Fortunately, the same thing goes for the solutions: we've been thinking about them for thousands of years. So much solace has been thought up! The first transformational centres are already starting to appear.

the house of early humanist Geert Groote: old principles find new meaning

space for reflection & re-envisioning

a Protestant church, featuring a Catholic cardinal and scientific Nobel Prize winners

PATIENT EMPOWERMENT
HEALING ENVIRONMENTS

What's the main similarity between a visit to a hospital and a visit to a museum? Both are experiences. Although people rarely go to the hospital to have a good time, it's no less important to inform, encourage, and inspire those visitors too. That's why we are seeing experiments with healing environments all across the globe, creating spaces that have a healthy and stimulating influence on people.

Magical wallpaper can be a source of joy for children. Moments of silence can serve the same purpose for adults. Finally, attractive passenger traffic areas improve everyone's mood, featuring anything from artsy interventions, games, or comic characters that join you as you move through the hospital and pop up when they're needed most.

And the effect is not only calming and soothing. Activating patients is key to their well-being and their recovery. Healthy habits, trained in playful environments are a first promising step.

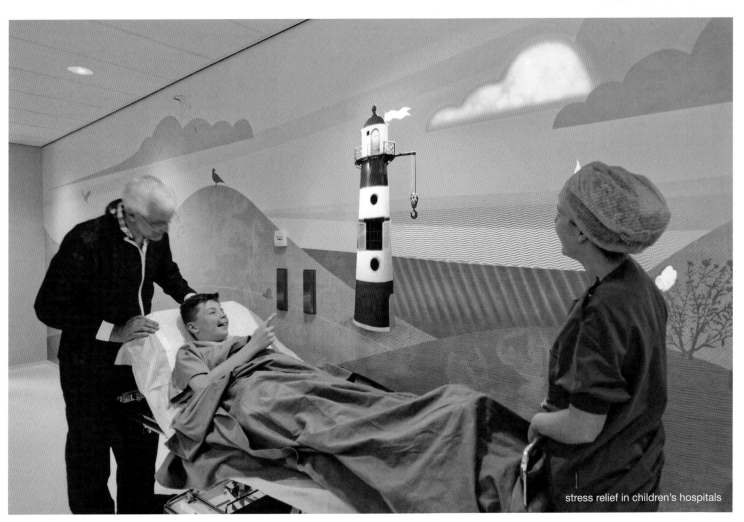

stress relief in children's hospitals

animated wallpaper shows buddies and band aid

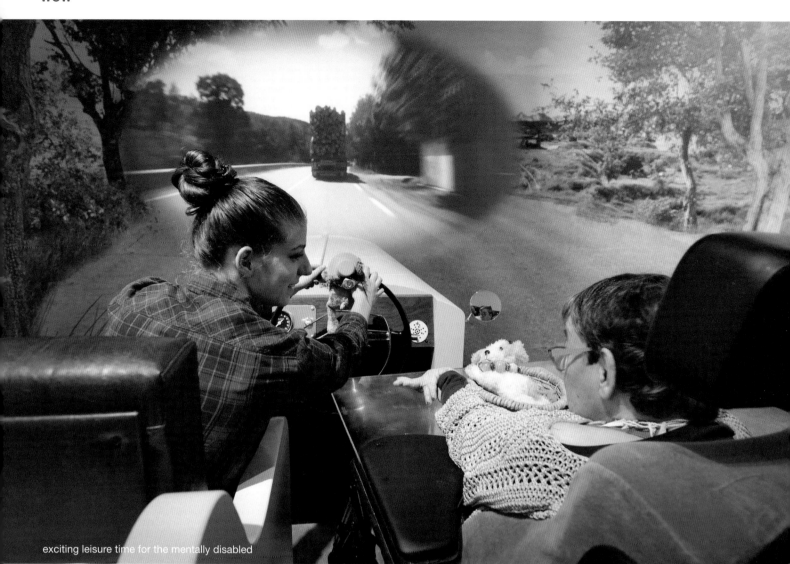

exciting leisure time for the mentally disabled

turning regular checks for overweight children into motivational play

SERIOUS PLAY

ADVENTUROUS ENVIRONMENTS FOR ALL AGES

Play is one of the fundamental ways in which we discover new realms. Fooling around in real life simulations – or in abstracted worlds, teaches you about your own behaviour – and that of others. Free play generates its own typical energy, in which you forget about time and the serious things you were occupied with.

Leisure centres have the key advantage that people visit them for fun. Nevertheless, their design is often serious and stiff. If you tease your visitors a little and don't always take yourself too seriously, you'll end up with a great space that visitors take possession of in a positive way. You provide them with the space and toys. The adventure starts when they take action

IRENE SIX
NAVAJO
POLICE SERGEANT
MELVIN BOEHME
TULALIP SNOHOMISH
CONGIERGE
ROY HAWTHORNE
NAVAJO
CODE TALKER
LAQUITA REUBEN
UMATILLA/NEZ PERCE
HIGH SCHOOL
EDDIE & MICHAEL
ONEIDA
BARBER & MECHANIC
LAKOTA SIOUX
ACTOR
DARRIN & ERIKA
NAVAJO
MUSICIAN & MOTHER
ASSINIBOINE
(GRAND)MOTHER
KELSEY LEONARD
SHINNECOCK
WATER RESOURCE ANALYST
PAMUNKEY

SEEING WITH NEW EYES

GENERATING NEW PERSPECTIVES

Changing your views can be one of the hardest things, even in the face of good indications that other perspectives could be more accurate. That, however, is exactly what many subjects need. Some stories have been told so often that there's hardly anything new in them at all. Some ideas have settled into our minds so deeply that a fresh, new approach is difficult to find. Times change, though, and so does the way people think. We're always discovering new facts about our history, and sometimes the present time requires us to adopt new norms and values.

Experience design is quite adept at handling this kind of challenge, because it's used to seeing things in a new light and to creating novel perspectives. It starts off with identifying who we are now, before providing inspiring alternatives that generate new understanding. It's like crawling inside someone else's mind and discovering what happens when you leave your comfort zone.

American Indians between myth and reality:
about stubborn stereotypes and real cultures

REVOLUSI
REVOLUSI

the story of the Dutch East Indies
and the impact on all those involved

war stories told by witnesses from five different countries

FROM MAGIC LANTERN TO VIRTUAL REALITY

CROSSOVER TECHNOLOGIES

Media technology provides us with access to worlds unknown. You can use it to travel to the future or into the mind of a surrealist artist. It lets you penetrate the innermost core of a Higgs Boson or the outer frontiers of the universe.

Imagine that the violin hadn't existed when Mozart was alive, or that oil paint hadn't been around for Rembrandt to use. Technology isn't there to compete with humankind, it's there to help us expand. It's a part of our evolution, defining our surroundings as well as our inner selves.

Technology is our *next nature*, allowing us to extend our senses. It enables us to zoom in and out, to stop or accelerate time and to see colours that are known to bees, but invisible to our own species. The best application of technology, however, is visualing things that do not exist yet: dreams, ideas and thoughts that can hardly be expressed in words.

The eyes are the mirror of the soul and media provide the canvas for our thoughts. From the most ancient cave drawings to the most recent renderings: people have always created images that tell stories in order to touch others. The latest generation of media creators plays with platforms as if they were blocks of Lego. Everything is connected and interaction is paramount.

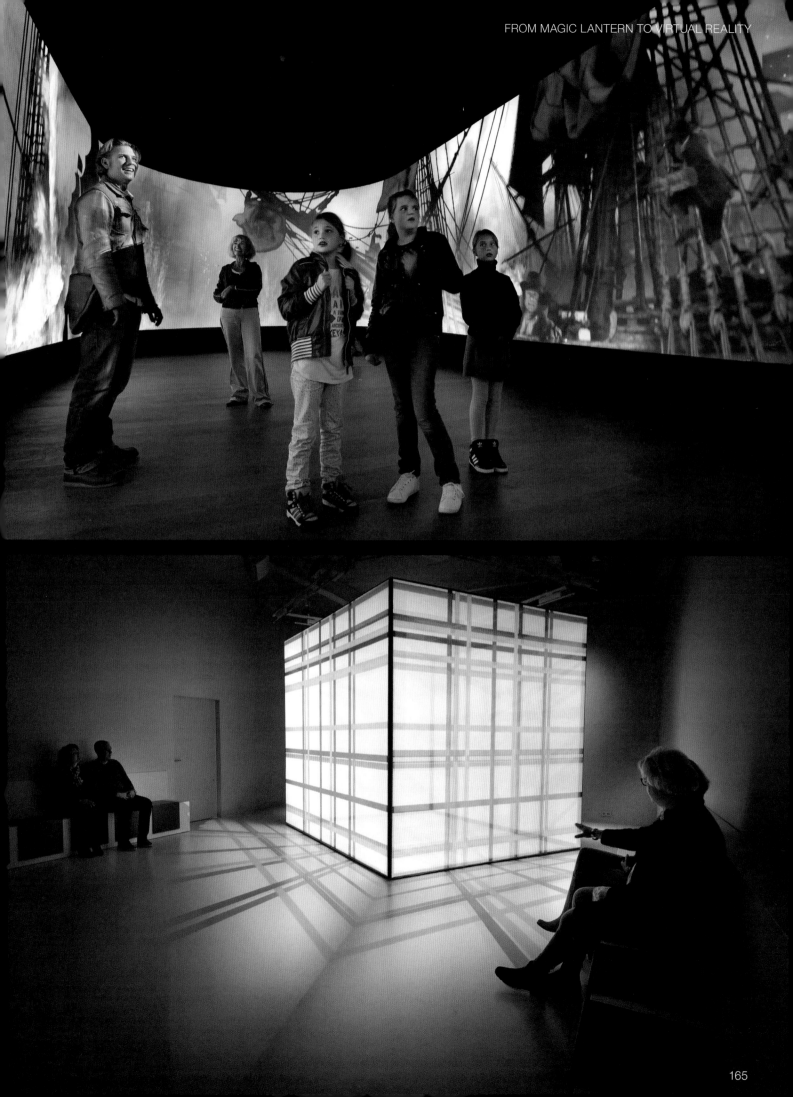

theatrum anatomicum magicum

MAKER SPACES
CREATIVE ZONES FOR PRACTICAL MINDS

There is a tinkerer in each of us. Who doesn't love discovering new things and combining existing ones to create something new? This works just as well with old radios as it does with new ideas. It involves fiddling with concepts in much the same way as a watchmaker tinkers with mechanisms.

The wealth of results this generates never ceases to amaze: it's as if there's a higher power in play. In fact, though, these results are entirely the product of the creative minds of the participants involved.

We call it serendipity: a combination of events that's too good to be entirely coincidental. This process can be organised: just turn your workplace into an adventure lab. Establish flexible rules with the tinkerers for a day. Let everything take care of itself and gratefully accept whatever results this yields.

Tinkering spaces come in all shapes and sizes, ranging from carefully organised spaces for just as carefully organised companies to pleasantly chaotic ones, if that's a better fit. The action is the experience.

prototyping tomorrow

ONTWERP EEN
ERTUIG ZONDER WIELEN

BEWEEG JE ZELF ZO
SNEL MOGELIJK VOORT
EERST NAAR VOREN,
DAN NAAR ACHTEREN

START!
0,00

inventing vehicles without wheels

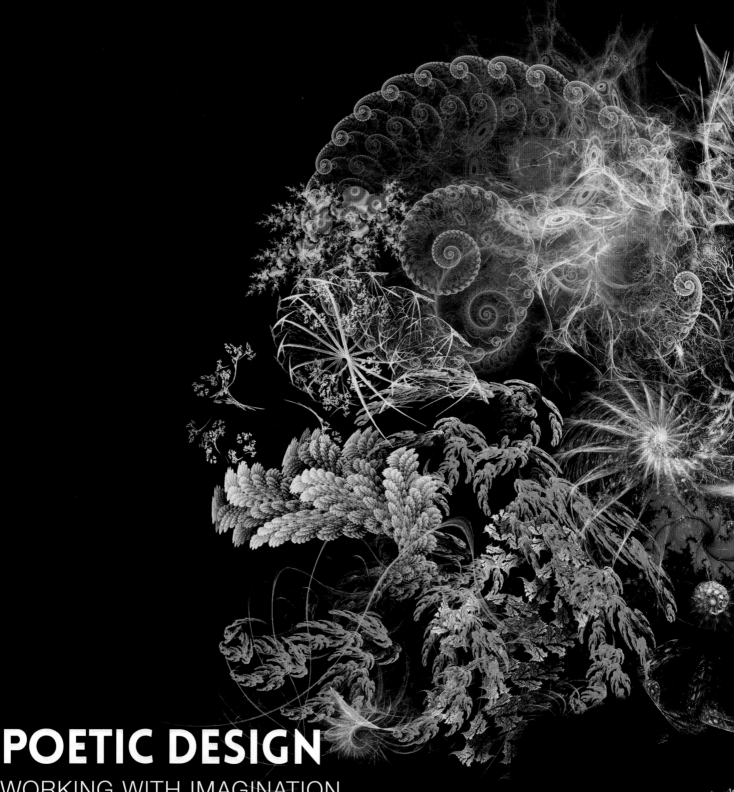

Don Tan 05

POETIC DESIGN
WORKING WITH IMAGINATION

A good dose of imagination can work wonders. Designing WoWs requires stretching our comfort zones to meet the Fantastic Unknown. Expressions that cannot be categorised immediately may seem odd at first, but also have the capacity to tease our minds and spark our senses. Imagination activates the audience to start engaging with the World of Wonder, to join in and fantasise.

Inspiration works in mysterious ways and some things only reveal their secrets once given proper attention and appreciation. Besides, the world already has plenty of serious communication in it: taking a poetic approach can be fun at times. Don't think about it too much, be prepared to let go and enjoy.

fractal formulas visualise the scientific tree of life

his and her silverware

corporate tree of life blooming with food wrapping flowers

4

A step-by-step plan for developing
a World of Wonder, from the initial
Big Idea to the snag list after opening.

HOW

4.1

THE BIG IDEA

Creating a World of Wonder starts with the initiative of turning a topic into an adventure. It goes without saying that a few requirements have to be met to get there. In what follows, we'll discuss the characteristics of the so-called Big Idea underlying all WoWs. We will also describe how you can develop such an idea in a team, by making use of an elegant creative thinking tool.

PURPOSE & POWER

In the context of this book, a Big Idea is a very short story that expresses why a particular experience centre should be developed, why it will have a magnetic pull on its intended visitors, what these visitors will experience, and how you are planning to achieve this. If all goes well, you won't need more than a single A4 page.

The purpose of a Big Idea is to fire up stakeholders, convincing them to devote their attention to your project. A strong *Why*, describing the reason that this new centre will make the world a better place, is of vital importance. A *Who*, indicating the people or organisation behind the idea, and a *What*, specifying the actual thing you're planning to develop, are equally indispensable. Having said that, ideas come in all shapes and sizes and not all of them are equally good. We can distinguish three factors that will determine whether yours will work.

IMAGINATIVE POWER

The word idea comes from the Greek *eidos*, which means 'that which is seen'. As such, Big Ideas are often visual documents, or must be written in visual language. The imaginative power is the visionary potential of the idea, highlighting the path towards the ideal. Idealism, vision, thinking big and optimism are a few welcome ingredients, but so are simplicity, a focus on the core issues and recognisability. If people can quickly understand and share your idea, there's a good chance it has enough imaginative power to succeed.

FORMATIVE POWER

A Big Idea provides a new perspective on a certain situation or sheds new light on a particular problem, making it a light, attractive issue. The formative power of an idea is its capacity to solve issues. If you're onto a good idea, it'll serve several distinct purposes, by benefiting the various stakeholders of the organisation in a number of ways, for instance. You can check whether your idea has sufficient formative power by listing all the purposes the centre serves for the hosts and visitors.

ACTIVATING POWER

To realise a Big Idea, parties with completely divergent interests must be inspired to act together. A good idea contains a call to action for all parties involved, which represents the activating power of the idea. You can check whether your idea has sufficient activating power by investigating whether several different parties are enthusiastic about actually carrying out the idea. The difference between formative power and activating power lies in the fact that the former pertains to functionality, whereas the second pertains to energy.

the capacity to envision

the capacity to solve

the capacity to mobilise

war and peace will meet in the new museum villa

HOW TO COME UP WITH BIG IDEAS

The three powers stated above give a pretty good indication of the strength of a Big Idea, as well as the likelihood that it'll work out for you. The question remains: how do you find one?
The creative method of 'thinking out of the box', a famous concept originating from the world of advertising before being co-opted by various other sectors, isn't entirely suitable for coming up with a good idea for a World of Wonder. That's because this technique mainly triggers associative thoughts, whereas WoWs require a more essentialist

approach. Their goal is to create awareness and engagement. In other words: you want to tell a striking story, which requires authenticity and honesty. You'll find it easier to think of ideas for this type of story with the opposite of 'thinking out of the box', or 'thinking inside the box'. It involves trying to get to the heart of the matter, including the critical parts that might not seem very appealing at first, such as resistance and mistakes that are related to the topic or the organisation behind it. You also look for truly

inspirational aspects, which go beyond everyday corporate interests, but that actually represent and realise the ultimate goal of the organisation. It's these two sides – taboo and glory, pain and pleasure, shadow and spirit – that make for an interesting story. A Big Idea reflects the entire picture, not just the pretty side.

THINKING INSIDE THE BOX

This is an easy framework for implementing thinking inside the box, which resembles a sort of natural creativity. We're sure that you're familiar with those great revelations about mundane problems that arise when you're taking a shower. The reason this happens, is because it's a moment of release: a different part of your brain takes over and comes up with a solution without

you interfering. This is the central moment of thinking inside the box. Before the revelation, your brain was hard at work to try and solve a problem. When you let the problem go, you discover something that had already been there all that time: a beautiful solution that puts everything in place. All you have to do afterwards is sit down and work it all out.

This rather intimate experience can be organised for larger groups, without having to take a shower together. There are five steps in this process: Analyse, Identify, Let Go, Envision and Specify. They represent two different mentalities that you will recognise from the shower-situation: the *ascending* mentality, analysing problems up to their ultimate essence, and the *descending* mentality of getting things grounded.

Most people have one of these two mindsets. Putting together an effective creative team depends on finding the right mix of both types, while ensuring there's plenty of room for playfulness and inspiration. All that's left is to have a conversation following these steps, bringing both mindsets to the table.

If you question inspired minds carefully enough, they'll become enormously intelligent: they'll do everything they can in order to protect and foster their creation.

ASCENDING
ANALYSE

This stage consists of analysing the assignment and the situation it describes. It starts off with the *Why & Who*: why should this destination be developed and who would visit it? Which relationships are there between the topic and the intended visitors? Why would they not already be familiar with the story? Which strategic goals will this initiative serve for the organisation developing it? Is there any resistance within the organisation to opening an experience centre? The analysis stage is finished once you have a complete picture of the subject and the intentions and wishes of the stakeholders, which includes the intended visitor/user.

ASCENDING
IDENTIFY

The second step consists of simplifying the initiative until there's no easier way to describe it any more. This compact description should contain all the aspects determined during the first step, but they must be extremely condensed and reduced to their essence. At this point, the main reason to set up the experience centre will become apparent, as agreed upon by everyone at the table.

TRANSITION
LET GO

At the transition between the ascending and descending group, we can insert a stage that involves 'taking a break and thinking about something else'. This is the shower moment. It's a moment of pleasure: a new mentality takes centre stage. It can be provoked by sending everyone home and/or buying them an ice cream. Why not try enjoying a great meal/film/walk together?

DESCENDING
ENVISION

In the fourth step, the assignment is articulated as an idea: the *What* is what matters here. If the analysis stage is performed properly and if the right team has been assembled, the core idea will now take shape, with all the ingredients specified in the assignment returning as elements of the idea. This is when you'll hear people say *"everything's falling into place."*

DESCENDING
SPECIFY

The final step concerns specification. After an idea has been developed, what often works well is carefully asking the most enthusiastic people: why will this manage to draw an audience? Who would sponsor this? How will the subject come to life? How can this idea be marketed attractively? What's the promise? If you question inspired minds carefully enough, they'll become enormously intelligent: they'll do everything they can in order to protect and foster their creation.

The process described above is common for people who have creative jobs. They often spend long periods brooding in seclusion, examining the subject from all angles. They'll also frequently focus on something completely different in an attempt to let the matter rest for a while: talented creatives mess around a lot. By the time they've come up with an idea, however, and you ask them about its value, they'll be hopelessly stubborn as they attempt to nourish and foster their creation. This process mirrors the five steps we just described.

IDEAS THAT FIT

Big Ideas developed by following this method have a key characteristic that distinguishes them from ideas developed in out-of-the-box sessions: they *fit*. Thanks to the robust analysis and specification, they are a perfect fit for the situation they're intended for. This is important, because they will serve as the source for all following developmental steps. The Big Idea has to activate a lot of parties, preferably in a coherent manner. In-the-box ideas are ideas that make you think: Of course! *Why haven't we thought of this before?* If you hear your sponsor exclaim these words, you're obviously on the right track.

The Big Idea is now ready to be framed, polished, immortalised and cast in bronze. Afterwards, it's flattened and rolled out into a long ribbon, completing its transformation into a *concept*. You can read more about this in the next chapter.

READ MORE
handboek voor hemelbestormers,
Stan Boshouwers, Dutch only.

expert sessions for the Museum of National History

4.2
CONCEPT DEVELOPMENT

The concept development phase is centred around operationalising the Big Idea. This involves determining the experience centre's main communicative objective and defining visitor flows plus visitor experiences. Moreover, this phase will also reveal the project requirements. Together, these elements make up the concept or project brief, a basic document that can be used by decision makers, designers, managers and fundraisers.

INTRO

Developing a Big Idea into a concept is a bit like a Big Bang: initially it doesn't have any dimensions in time and space, but that's what the concept phase is for. This phase constitutes a number of steps specifying all the dimensions of the concept: writing a synopsis and profiling the target audiences (1D), charting the visitor flow on a map (2D), determining the visitor experience in each space (3D) and plotting the visitor journey in time (4D). In addition to this, the project requirements will also become apparent. We'll walk you through each of the above steps in the same order that you'll typically find in practice.

1D
SYNOPSIS

A synopsis is actually a flattened Big Idea being put in a linear timeline that the future visitor will navigate (hence 1D). Depending on the scope of the project, this adventure either starts at home or at the front door of the visitor centre.

It should contain a short but comprehensive description of the experience including at least:
– the place of action
– the adventure in a nutshell
– the relevance of the story
– a list of subjects and/or characters with corresponding emotions.

It is also important to carefully specify the who, why and what more extensively. Who is going to be visiting the centre and why, and what this person will ultimately take home.

It's often possible to distinguish between various visitor groups that each have their own reasons and motivations. These constitute the Why of their visit.
When identifying them, you can differentiate between:

REASON TO KNOW
Why would they know about you?

REASON TO GO
Why would a visit be in their interest?

REASON TO GROW
Which 'life purpose' do you serve? Why will a visit help your visitors to grow? What do they dream of?

REASON TO SHARE
Why would they share their experience? And how do you ensure this?

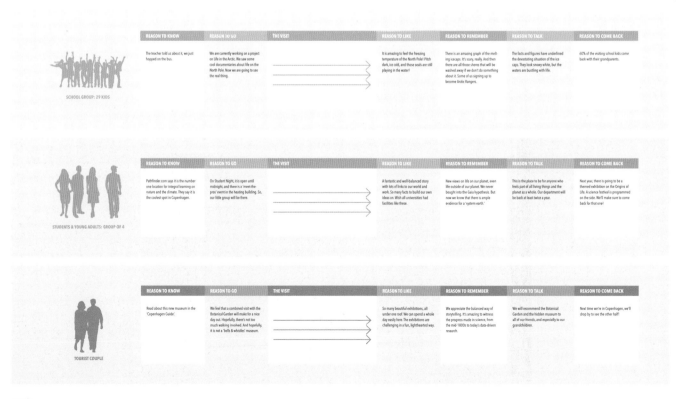

2D
VISITOR FLOW

This step involves applying the synopsis to the available space. It can be considered 2D because you'll be making a map of both the themes involved and the route that visitors will take to encounter them in the proper order. This routing is something that also concerns the architect.

The two expertises meet when it comes to *visitor flow*: the way people move through the building. Architects can tell you everything about flux, capacity and the dimensions required. The experience designer will be adding their know-how about the rhythms of attention, energy, sharing and reflection that visitors will experience as they flow through the space.

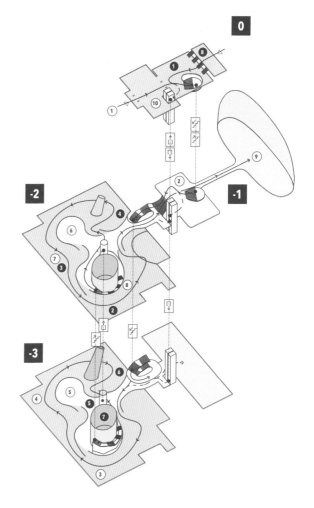

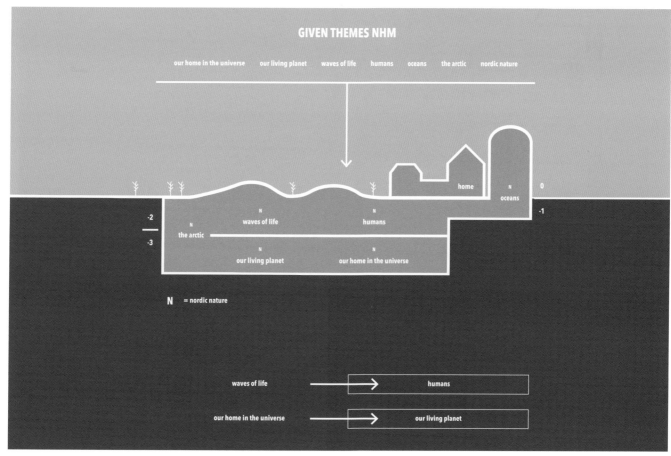

3D
VISITOR EXPERIENCE

The visitor experience represents the description and visualisation of what happens to people and where it takes place. Because this means you'll be translating the synopsis and flow into a spatial dimension, we can call it 3D. Imagination comes first, letting stakeholders form a picture of what the experience centre will have to offer when it's completed.

This isn't a design yet, merely a series of *impressions* that can be compared with a storyboard for a movie. In addition, it will shed light on how to properly frame the focus for your visitors: which aspect of the message do you want them to pay attention to? The way the overall storyline is structured is important, but this part of the concept also

allows you to express more emotional aspects of the experience: how does it feel and what does it evoke? Identifying the right associations at this stage helps you to improve the impact of your designs afterwards.

2

3

conceptualising the new Natural History Museum of Denmark

4D
VISITOR JOURNEY

The next step involves combining all the aspects so far into a single, coherent visitor journey. This describes the adventure that your visitors will experience, including its intended purpose, main steps, types of experiences, routing and timing (hence 4D). It can be helpful to keep the principles of journey design (chapter 1.6) in mind during this process, because it will provide a framework for your WoW and the elements that appear in it:

1. INVITATION
How do your guests find out about the adventure?
Which obstacles do they have to overcome before visiting?

2. TRANSITION
What is the appeal, what kind of welcome is there, which adventure are you promising?

3. INTRODUCTION
How do you get your visitors into the right mind set?
What is the atmosphere in your World of Wonder?

4. EXPLORATION
Which topics are covered?
Which activities can be developed?
How do you challenge and engage people?

5. ADMIRATION
What is the beautiful side of the story?
How can you evoke awe?

6. IMMERSION
What is the highlight of the experience?
What insight do visitors get there?

7. CONNECTION
In which ways can the visitors connect with the subject?
How do you make it personal?

8. RECOLLECTION
How does the adventure end?
What kind of surrounding facilities are there?

9. INTEGRATION
What will the visitors take home?
What will the visit give them?

VISITOR A:
NATHAN
2.5 HOUR VISIT

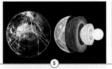

1 I take a walk through the Botanical Garden. I come here often and enjoy the nineteenth-century greenhouses and the old museum buildings. I used to visit the Geological Museum from time to time. I love the tranquillity of the place, and I admire the fact that they still organize temporary exhibitions. I enter the new museum through the former theater building. It is really well done! A nice, open room where history fits in seamlessly with the modern times.

2 After buying a day ticket, I go down the stairs. I get to an intermediate floor that grants a spectacular view of a curving underground square. But before going there, I take a look at the maps on the wall that illustrate how this special building has been put together and where I can find what. I decide on the chronological route, starting from the Big Bang and finishing with the arrival of man. I'm quite excited!

3 I go down two levels and find myself in another underground square. The corridors are not crowded, and I get the feeling that I am on a voyage of discovery. I feel like a speleologist, but that's just my imagination, of course. At the far end of the square, I see a gigantic globe with floating land masses. I go over to take a look and see that this is a show about the formation of the earth. It's quite a sensation to see four and a half billion years of history pass by in four and a half minutes. I want to find out more and walk into the exhibition that accompanies it.

4 In 'Our Home in the Universe', I learn that the Big Bang wasn't Big at all - there was no distance - nor was there a Bang - there was no sound. I do see a fascinating exhibition that explains how the theories about the early beginnings of the universe have been researched. My own university is part of that research, which I didn't know. There are parts I don't understand, so I copy a link to my phone. This will allow me to read up on the topic at home. I definitely want to learn more about it.

5 A little further down, I see another model of our globe. You can see that the earth has a solid inner core, which I knew already. Hey, there's a portrait of Inge Lehmann, my fellow-Dane, and it says that she is the one who discovered this. I'm surprised to learn that she concluded that the inner core is solid on the basis of her analysis of seismic wave measurements. With hindsight, it seems easy... It's a brilliant story.

6 I have come back to the inner square, one floor up this time. I sit at ease by a small lake, with animals and a human being drinking from it. If I look down into the spring, I see the globe that I looked at earlier. This really is an extraordinary building. The view through gets me thinking about the levels of our knowledge and about the earth as a source of life. I try to decipher what the intentions are, and it brings a smile to my face. Now I understand what they are looking for, especially with the arrival of the Anthropocene.

7 I did know how the dinosaurs became extinct. But I never realised that there were four mass extinctions before then. It is hard to imagine that the oceans coloured pink, purple, or even black during the first one - due to hydrogen sulphide emissions, apparently. 95% of marine life and 70% of life on land just died from a shortage of oxygen!

8 While I wander around the biodiversity exhibition, I notice some movement on the wall. It's subtle, but it's there. When I walk over, I see the large realms of biology: the archaea, bacteria, eukaryotes, plants, animals, and fungi. I was aware of the classification, but it is always fascinating to see how our biomass is ordered. Almost all of them are single-celled! Never before have I been such a clear explanation of the formation of the biosphere.

9 I was getting a little tired, but in the Oceans' Hall, I'm wide awake again. Such a wonderful room! After the long corridor, it feels like a true discovery. I start by checking out the glass cases, in which marine life has been represented artfully. Every glass case covers a different ecosystem. The term 'glass case' does not do them justice. They are a mixture of glass case, aquarium, and diorama. They show me what a mysterious domain the oceans are. There are a few things that we know, and these fragments can be seen. But there is so much more that we don't know yet.

10 After fifteen minutes, I sit down in the centre of the hall. The soundless shadow play on the ceiling that has given me an ocean-like feel changes into a larger show. I put on headphones, and I can choose between different speakers, who all give their own vision on life. Their stories cover the origin of life, its inconceivable resilience, and the established fact that we're all made from stardust. While they tell me so, I see the most wonderful animated forms over my head. The slats of the building wave, and I see the blue whale, gigantic and helpless at the same time. It moves me to see how life goes on, in one huge flow. It's something to take good care of.

PROJECT REQUIREMENTS

Besides all the creative stuff, there are also a number of practical requirements that need to be defined for the project to work out smoothly. These are crucial for both an effective process and an effective result. During this phase, these prerequisites or conditions can still be high level, but they need to be refined in later stages.

The most straightforward ones:

BUDGET
What is the experience centre allowed to cost?

PLANNING
Within what time frame should the experience centre be realised?

PARTNERS
Which stakeholders will be involved and how will each contribute?

CONTEXT
What is the framework for this project?

4	14	30	74	86	88
CONCEPT	EXPERIENCE	DESIGN	PRODUCTION	BUDGET	ATTACHMENTS

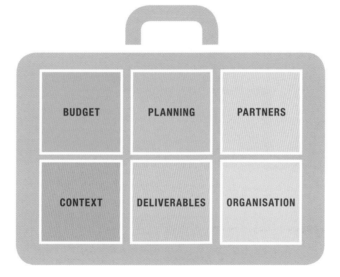

BUDGET · PLANNING · PARTNERS · CONTEXT · DELIVERABLES · ORGANISATION

BUSINESS CASE

The concept is often used for internal or external fundraising, which means that having clear financial underpinnings is crucial. This applies to any investments made, as well as to operating the centre. In the concept, a rough indication of the budget is often enough, as are the operational principles of the centre, potential revenue streams and eligible sponsors. One way to estimate the total investment is based on square metre prices (see ch. 4.7). Another option is to compare your centre to others. If the business case forms the most important part of the concept, it can also be referred to as a feasibility study. If the experience centre will serve as a component of a larger spatial programme, it could be part of a more comprehensive master plan.

THE PROMISE

One of the main outcomes of the concept development stage is the intended qualitative results of the experience centre, also known as the *promise*. This is a joint statement by all parties, in which they agree on the desired effect of the project, in terms of a message, experience or change in behaviour. This promise is important for the relationship between the investors, designers and builders, as it establishes a number of key rules and principles during the design and construction process. In some cases, the parties draw up a separate list of the most important points. If the project comes under pressure – which it always will – these foundations and agreements can serve as a guide to keep the project on course. In addition, the parties involved can agree to appoint a *Chief Promise* to monitor their ambitions. He or she will be in charge of quality control throughout the project. This is a major role, since carefully managing time and money will often take centre stage later on. This person may be the art director or also a client representative.

Now, if you write down and illustrate all these elements, collect them and present them nicely, you'll have a concept that can be understood by a wide range of professionals. When printed, this is often called a bid book, which aims to get people interested in your plan. They may include stakeholders who need to be convinced by its impact, or sponsors that might want to fund the project. In day-to-day practice, we develop a huge number of these concepts, master plans and bid books for a wide range of clients who seek to turn their ideas into reality. Once this next stage starts, the concept serves another purpose still: being an anchor of sorts for all design and construction phases.

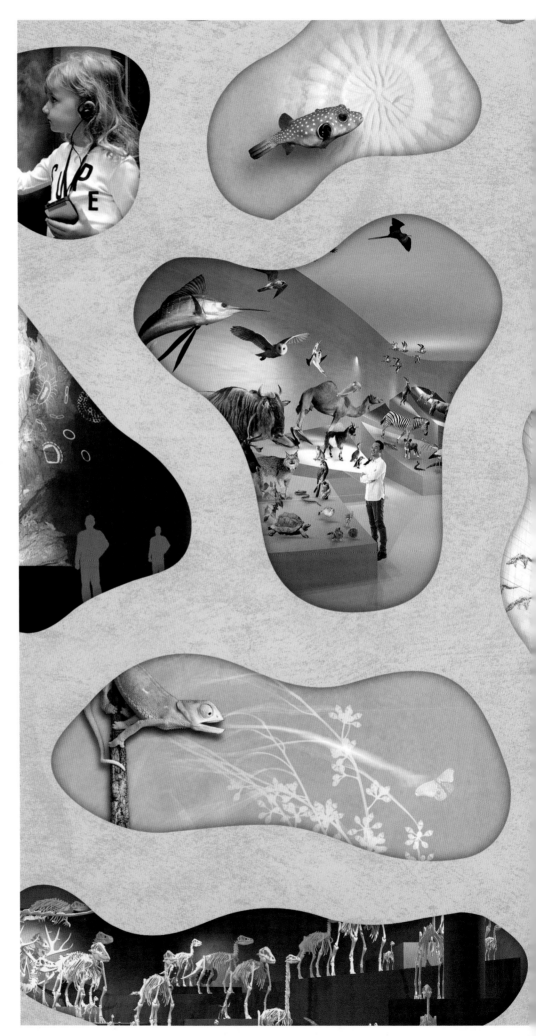

SUMMARY

You might structure the concept as follows:

0. THE INTRODUCTION
The introduction summarises why this project is important.

1. BIG IDEA
The first chapter is the Big Idea, highlighted in words and pictures, letting everyone see how appealing it will be.

2. TARGET AUDIENCE
The target audience specifies the intended visitors to the centre, as well as the need it can fulfil.

3. VISITOR JOURNEY
The visitor journey shows how the story is told and specifies the key moments. It's comprised of a series of sketches of spatial situations that will tell people reading the concept what can be experienced in the centre.

4. PROJECT REQUIREMENTS
The project requirements specify the business conditions with which the project must comply. This chapter can contain a 'milestone' planning.

5. BUSINESS CASE
The business case explains the underlying financial plan and identifies potential sponsors (specific cases can be included as a separate document due to confidentiality issues and sponsorships that haven't quite been locked down yet).

6. FOLLOW-UP STEPS
A concept often concludes with a list of follow-up steps.

These next steps start with a thorough planning. That is the subject of the next chapter.

4.3 PLANNING

The building or site that houses an experience centre has a major influence on how people perceive their visit, which is why it is important that they are developed harmoniously. The following describes a plan of work that synchronises the development of both, whilst complying with international standards. The phases addressed here can also be implemented if the centre and the site are not developed simultaneously. Together, they sum up the main steps of developing a World of Wonder.

SYNCHRONISING PROJECT FLOWS

In part 3, we explained the relationship between buildings and exhibitions. The building acts as an envelope for the experience. The spaces within the building form the scenographic layer in which Worlds of Wonder take shape. This layer can differ for every room, so that visitors, as in a movie, can end up in different scenes or acts of the story. Museography accounts for the third layer, where the story is told by means of objects, stories and challenges. Naturally, these three elements must be linked closely to each other: even though they're created by different designers (architects don't design exhibitions and exhibition designers definitely won't design a building), the visitor experiences the three distinct designs as one. They enter a single experiential world, and the greater its coherence and expressive capacity, the more impact the visit will have. As such, developing the building and exhibition at the same time is an incredibly good idea.

Even though it's important, it doesn't always happen, primarily because architecture is usually the first step of construction projects. The architect may designate certain rooms to 'the experience', but because no one knows what that will actually be, the parties that devise the actual experience are typically a rather late addition to the process, which comes at the cost of great opportunities for impactful design. However, we also have to admit that professional egos can get in the way. To put it negatively, for once: some architects prefer there to be as few objects as possible in their building, especially if their presence would lead to new scenes within their world.

Sure, people are allowed to enter, but apart from that they'd like to see gallery-like rooms with as little clutter as possible. On the other hand, some experience designers prefer dark boxes without any natural daylight, allowing them to stay in control of the entire experience. Without natural light, after all, artificial light is king, effectively turning the room into a theatre or studio. Such an approach negates architecture, which is no less a missed opportunity.

Of course, there are also examples to be found of architecture and interior design reinforcing each other. In those cases, the building contributes to telling the story, with the scenography highlighting the strengths of the architecture. The starting point is a simple one: the impact of a visit is expressed in a common language that allows architects and designers to talk to each other, which makes it a lot easier to achieve their common goal: creating an unforgettable visit.

Synchronising the development of the building and its interior helps to answer some typical planning questions: When to do what? How to cut up the creative process into manageable chunks? How to project & control spending? And above all: what is the opening date?

THE RIBA PLAN OF WORK

Because buildings literally envelop Worlds of Wonder, we'll align our-selves to the phases of the architectural process. There are international standards for this process, such as the RIBA Plan of Work. RIBA is the abbreviation of the Royal Institute of British Architects, but its use is by no means restricted to the UK. Their model organises the process of briefing, designing, constructing, maintaining, operating and using building projects into a number of key stages. These stages are represented in the columns of the upper table on this page, reprinted with the kind permission of RIBA. The rows consist of so-called 'Task Bars': various types of activities that will be completed during the process by different

specialists. There are numerous bars available for specialisms such as procurement, legal affairs, sustainability issues, etcetera. Users just click on the bars they need and off it goes. The Plan of Work is a great support tool for interdisciplinary projects, because it allows everyone involved to understand the tasks performed by other parties in any given phase. Moreover, it specifies which party delivers what in which phase, allowing the other parties to build upon that information.

In what follows, we will look through the lens of RIBA, even if the planned centre will occupy a pre-existing building or the WoW will be an outdoor affair.

RIBA Plan of Work 2013	Stages	0 Strategic Definition
Tasks ▼		
Core Objectives		Identify client's **Business Case** and **Strategic Brief** and other core project requirements.
Procurement *Variable task bar		Initial considerations for assembling the project team.
Programme		Establish Project Programme

EXPERIENCE DESIGN TASK BAR

Entirely on our own authority, we have added an extra task bar to the RIBA Plan of Work, called the *Experience Design Task Bar*. Vertically, this provides an overview of the different phases of the experience design process and how they relate to the architectural phases. This allows us to show how the two disciplines can be synthesised into similar assignments.

Horizontally, we summarise the core tasks and objectives of the experience design process for the key tracks of story development, design and cost control.

This will all be dealt with in more detail in the upcoming chapters. For now the key focus lies on the planning itself, specifying clear outcomes for every phase.

When the initiative for a WoW is launched, the planning will only contain a single key entry: the opening date. The investors look forward to that moment, because for the board, it's the date that matters most. In the following steps, the types of planning between the project launch and the opening moment are specified.

Experience Design Task Bar	Phases	0 Big Idea
Tasks ▼		
Storytelling		initial project description
Design		creative vision
Planning		opening date
Cost Control		budget class determined

The RIBA Plan of Work 2013 organises the process of briefing, designing, constructing, maintaining, operating and using building projects into a number of key stages. The content of stages may vary or overlap to suit specific project requirements. The RIBA Plan of Work 2013 should be used solely as guidance for the preparation of detailed professional services contracts and building contracts.

www.ribaplanofwork.com

1 Preparation and Brief	2 Concept Design	3 Developed Design	4 Technical Design	5 Construction	6 Handover and Close Out	7 In Use
Develop **Project Objectives**, including **Quality Objectives** and **Project Outcomes**, **Sustainability Aspirations**, **Project Budget**, other parameters or constraints and develop **Initial Project Brief**. Undertake **Feasibility Studies** and review of **Site Information**.	Prepare **Concept Design**, including outline proposals for structural design, building services systems, outline specifications and preliminary **Cost Information** along with relevant **Project Strategies** in accordance with **Design Programme**. Agree alterations to brief and issue **Final Project Brief**.	Prepare **Developed Design**, including coordinated and updated proposals for structural design, building services systems, outline specifications, **Cost Information** and **Project Strategies** in accordance with **Design Programme**.	Prepare **Technical Design** in accordance with **Design Responsibility Matrix** and **Project Strategies** to include all architectural, structural and building services information, specialist subcontractor design and specifications, in accordance with **Design Programme**.	Offsite manufacturing and onsite **Construction** in accordance with **Construction Programme** and resolution of **Design Queries** from site as they arise.	Handover of building and conclusion of **Building Contract**.	Undertake **In Use** services in accordance with **Schedule of Services**.
Prepare **Project Roles Table** and **Contractual Tree** and continue assembling the project team.	← - - - The procurement strategy does not fundamentally alter the progression of the design or the level of detail prepared at a given stage. However, **Information Exchanges** will vary depending on the selected procurement route and **Building Contract**. A bespoke **RIBA Plan of Work 2013** will set out the specific tendering and procurement activities that will occur at each stage in relation to the chosen procurement route. - - - →			Administration of **Building Contract**, including regular site inspections and review of progress.	Conclude administration of **Building Contract**.	

1 Concept Development	2 Concept Design	3 Developed Design (preliminary/scheme design)	4 Final Design (detailed design)	5 Production	6 Handover	7 Operation
synopsis & interpretation strategy	narrative development & collection selection	working out storylines & collection plan	content & collection diagram, AV & MM scripts	copy, AV / MM production	delivery of all AV / MM media and texts	updates
visitor journey & design principles	sketching main scenes, visual & spatial identity	design of spaces, displays, exhibits and media	detailed drawings for production, prototyping	off-site manufacturing and on-site installation	site acceptance tests	updates
phasing	milestone planning	detailed planning	production planning	installation planning	snag lists	service & maintenance
budget breakdown	estimated item list	calculated item list	value engineering, contracts with suppliers	execution of contracts, contingencies	delivery of goods	depreciation of exhibitions

MASTER PROJECT PLANNING

During concept development (corresponding to *RIBA 1: Preparation and Brief*) the principal plan is made, aligning phases from the building project to the experience design project. During concept design, a milestone plan is made, specifying deadlines for things such as funding, signing off on designs, and having the building ready for use. During developed design, a detailed plan is made by the lead project manager specifying all deliverables for all parties in the following steps of the process. A precise demarcation is established, differentiating between items belonging to the architect and the experience designer, as well as a planning procedure for developing a consistent storyline, based on deliveries from both client organisation and the design department or agencies involved. In short: the design steps that follow will be all about the deliverables.

This does not mean, however, that planning is finished by now. Planning is always one phase ahead, so, during final design a detailed *production plan* is made, saying who will deliver what to whom and when this will happen. Think of programming apps, AV footage shot in the right season that then has to be post-produced, storyline details that all parties have agreed upon and cleared intellectual rights for using images and other artwork, to name just a few things. At the end of the final design phase, an installation plan is made, specifying the numerous parties that will shape the WoW. Apart from installing hardware and scenographic items, this involves show programming, theatre lighting and graphical signing, to name a few. A complex process that has its own strict order of steps.

A FARCE OF FIXTURES

There's a well-known anecdote in the design sector: you've spent the morning taking part in an in-depth exploratory session about the core values of the museum or company that has ordered a WoW, delving into the fundamental reasons for its existence and the way it ultimately wants to contribute to society. By going through this process, you hope that, together with the board, you'll find the starting points that can be used to design it. After a few hours, the session is over and the air is full of new insights and promising ideas for the future.

As you're about to leave, though, the project manager quickly calls out, asking you where the power outlets should be placed: *"It might be a hard question to answer at this stage, but the contractor really needs to know this afternoon..."* This is why Worlds of Wonder are so often organised around fixed data and electricity grids.

PLANNING YOUR WOW

As mentioned before, even if there is no building process to align with, these planning steps bear relevance. Actually, they are quite universal. Above you see a general plan for developing an experience centre, if you isolate it from real-estate issues. It all starts with a high-level initiative called a *Big Idea*. This is operationalised into a *concept*, which involves framing it into a feasible project proposal, including planning and budget requirements.

Then, after a nerve-wrecking Go/No-Go moment, the plan might be carried out. In that case, the project branches out into four main tracks, two of which are managerial and two are creative in nature: planning and cost control are usually carried out by the same department or project manager. Storytellling and design are different métiers, although they are closely intertwined. We will deal with that later.

In the next chapter we will take a look at the many jobs that are to be fulfilled when building a WoW.

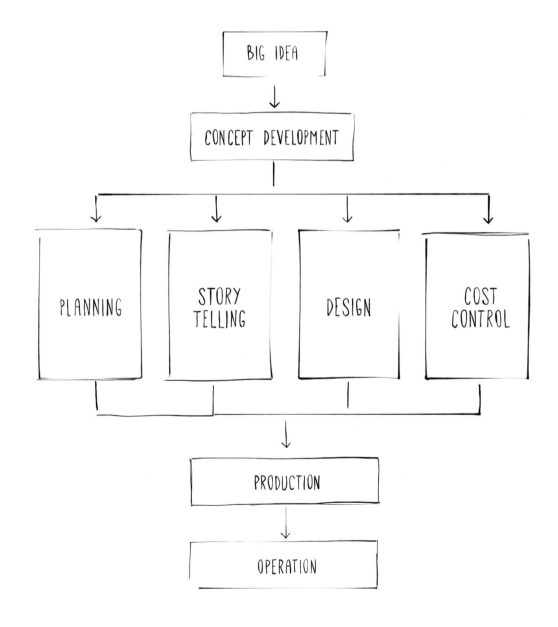

4.4
THE EXPERIENCE DESIGN TEAM

If the concept developed in the previous stages manages to find support, there's a good chance that the experience centre will ultimately be created. Now it's time to divide the tasks. Experience design is a multidisciplinary enterprise that brings together several fields of creative expertise. We'll now explain what these fields are and what role they have to play. The division of labour is considerable here. In smaller projects however, multiple jobs might be assigned to one and the same person.

EXPERIENCE DIRECTOR

It's up to the experience director to look at the design through the lens of the future visitor. You can take that quite literally: just like a film director, they have to coordinate all other creatives in the team to ensure that the centre provides its visitors with a powerful, unambiguous experience. This person is tasked with monitoring the coherence of the centre's media, the rhythm of the experience and the dosage of information. The experience director bears ultimate responsibility for achieving the communication goals and they'll often have played a role in specifying them.

When setting up the project, this person helps to think of ways in which the story can be conveyed in the most appealing manner possible. During the rest of the process, he or she safeguards the chosen strategy, which involves keeping both the creatives and the clients on track: if the focus of the project should gradually change during the process, this team member will be the one to point it out. This is closely related to the role of *Chief Promise*.

Another focus lies on the integration of all design disciplines into one coherent composition. This evolves around consistent quality control during development and production stages. This is also known as art direction.

CREATIVE CONSULTANT

Some might call this role that of strategist or concept developer, but we prefer creative consultant: someone who combines thorough analysis with creative imagination. This person is in charge of formulating the Interpretation Strategy of the experience centre. They look at the brief provided by investors and initiators, research the perceptions of the intended visitors and devise an effective visitor journey. The creative consultant is tasked with revealing the deeper motives of the client and its customers –the visitors– translating them into a creative approach. Accordingly, this person has to be involved with the process at an early stage.

The Interpretation Strategy is an agreement between the client and the creative agency (see chapter 4.5). Because they both consist of many different individual players, who can have varying interests and/or tastes, commitment is a key precondition for success. The creative consultant must understand the interests of all stakeholders and consider how these interests can be satisfied.

STORY DEVELOPER

The story developer ensures that the message is translated into a captivating narrative. They are in charge of elaborating the storylines mentioned in the concept. To this end, they are tasked with managing the content and ensuring that all of its components end up in the right place. They're focused on both the *narrative structure* (which subject is positioned where?) and the *narrative mode* (how is the story told?).

This means that the story developer is also in charge of where and how objects are positioned. In experience design, objects often take up the role of main characters in a story. This person is in charge of managing this story, putting the objects on stage at just the right time.

In addition, they direct the creative content producers such as audiovisual or multimedia designers. Their media content is part of the total narrative and it's up to the story developer to make sure it features exactly the right tone of voice and meaning. If the project so requires, this team member is supported by a content manager, who is in charge of identifying and sourcing potential content, and who directs content sharing between all persons involved, including the client.

ARCHITECTURAL LIAISON

One member of the imagineering team is in charge of maintaining the relationship with the architect and construction manager. This person has to ensure that the building and the exhibition reinforce each other, which is to say that they both contribute to the visitor experience in a coherent way. This role is especially important since – as we noted before – architects and experience designers do not necessarily speak each other's language. The core task of this team member is to synchronise the creative intentions and implications on both sides. The architectural liaison shares the plans drawn up by the designers and architects and translates the wishes of one party so that they can be understood by the other.

During the earlier design stages, he or she will research the flow of visitors through the building, charting their experience in the process. This revolves around organisation and spatial proportions, as well as atmosphere, daylight access, rhythm and materials used.

At the later stages of the construction process, the architectural liaison is in charge of sharing technical information and of integrating the experience design process into the building construction process.

2D DESIGNER

2D or graphic designers bring cohesion and identity to a World of Wonder. Since the process involves multiple creatives seeking to communicate a message with visitors in all sorts of ways, guaranteeing balance and recognisability can be a challenge. 2D designers are tasked with developing a spatial visual identity that lets visitors make sense of all the individual experiences by means of a clear and attractive framework.

This doesn't just relate to the graphical layer of the experience, but also to the implementation of artwork and photography, digital interfaces, routing, spatial text use and – of paramount importance – to the relationship with the visual

identity outside the centre. The website, adverts, and educational materials will be often produced by several different parties, but ultimately, they'll be part of a single experience for visitors.

2D designers are also involved in the communication of content. Together with the story developer, they'll look at which information is presented where and at how this is done. Thanks to this collaboration, the story will be told in carefully determined chunks and in a recognisable style.

3D DESIGNER

The 3D designer creates the world in which the adventure will take place. In the design team, it's up to this person to design the various scenes of the experience, which is why this person can also be called a Scenographer. He or she is in charge of determining the *look and feel* of a certain space, which strongly influences its credibility and eventual impact.

Another task is the positioning of media, exhibits and collections. As opposed to a stage or movie set, visitors are allowed to browse and wander around, so the touchpoints of the journey all need to be in the right place and style. What is their functionality, which elements do they consist of, and how does the visitor

engage with them? In later stages, there is an increasing focus on materiality and technicalities. All these elements will have an influence on the visitor experience and must be accurately modelled by the 3D designer.

AUDIOVISUAL DESIGNER

The AV designer is the team member who brings Worlds of Wonder to life by means of audiovisual media. You could see televisions, smart-phones and other screens as portals within the experience centre that lead, temporarily, to an alternate reality. Audiovisual designers create frame stories by means of movies, video installations and video mapping. More and more opportunities and possibilities are now arising rapidly: wandering around in an arcade-like world scattered with touchscreens is hardly a magical experience any-more, as this is no different than the world we live in. In Worlds of Wonder, the main part of the audiovisual experience takes place beyond the borders of a screen.

WoWs increasingly contain video paintings, where the main story and sub-stories blend into one another. New media technology has enabled experience designers to create completely animated worlds. Through techniques such as video mapping, audiovisual layers can literally be superimposed over the physical environment, which lets visitors undergo a joint, immersive experience.

It's important to note that the audiovisual component of an experience need not necessarily be overwhelming. The overall magic of a story is often enhanced by very subtle effects. It's the job of the AV designer to determine which approach will work best.

INTERACTION DESIGNER

Any World of Wonder worth its salt contains challenges, obstacles, games and rewards: this is where the inter-action designer comes into play. They have to look at the narrative space as an interface between a story and the visitors, who aren't just given a passive experience, but a task to complete as well. The interface lets visitors accomplish this task and enrich their experience as a result. Accordingly, the interaction designer plays a key role in activating visitors and helping them navigate the centre.

Interactions come in all shapes and sizes and can differ greatly in scope: they can be used as touchscreens or multimedia tables, to display content.

However, a more playful approach often works better. Principles and techniques taken from the gaming industry are increasingly used in media and spatial environments, with digital interfaces being replaced by physical interaction.

Finally, the space itself can be turned into a gaming environment, which means that when visitors interact with it, it will change and adapt accordingly. This is a great technique for so-called open game situations, which don't have rules to start with, but consist entirely of trying to discover these rules.

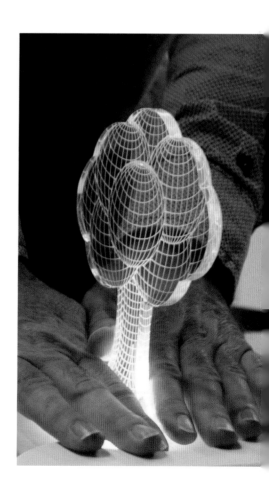

LIGHTING DESIGNER

Every designer and filmmaker knows that light makes or breaks an experience. It has a role to play at the level of the exhibition, where it literally highlights objects and automatically directs your visitors' attention to what you want to say. At the same time, light is also of major scenographic importance. Theatrical lighting brings people in the right mood and can create beautiful or meaningful effects.

For lighting designers, black boxes are an ideal situation, because it gives them complete control. This situation avoids the damaging effects that direct daylight can have on collections and on an interesting presentation.

Over the past decades, therefore, dark settings were fairly common, an approach that originates from the world of theatre.

Daylight, however, is also important, because it keeps people active. In large environments in particular, where visitors are supposed to spend several hours, natural light is critical to keep the visitors on their toes. The lighting designer must be a master of maintaining this balance. As with audiovisual materials, lighting need not be overly dramatic to be effective. Light is something you're usually unaware of, but which has a great influence on how and what we perceive.

SOUND DESIGNER

Sound has started playing an increasingly important role in the design mix. In the past, this wasn't the case in the world of museum design, where audio would mainly be played through headphones. As is the case for virtual reality, this comes at the expense of a group experience. In movies and theatre performances sound plays a different role altogether. Music, sound effects, voices and even the acoustics of a scene are subject to careful direction. You've probably watched a silent movie before, which only emphasises how great an influence audio has on the narrative and, as such, on the experience as a whole.

The sound designer is responsible for all these elements. This involves conveying content, for example through voice-overs and creating the right ambiance through so-called soundscapes. These are compositions of sounds and/or music that set the stage for the story to be told and that are carefully tailored to the experience.

Finally, it's up to the sound designer to ensure that audio is used in a balanced way throughout the experience. As with all other elements of an experience centre, sound works best when the highs and lows are carefully organised and coordinated.

OTHER SPECIALISTS

Other specialists often join the design table every now and then, adding specific expertise. These specialists represent fields such as feasibility research, marketing & branding, hardware design, accessibility, hygiene & safety, hospitality, education and building management. It is wise to involve them at an early stage to maximise their contribution. Under the guidance of the experience director, these experts ensure that the ultimate experience is a coherent one and check that the entire centre can be built within the project requirements.

PROJECT MANAGER

All these disciplines are coordinated by the project manager. This person is primarily responsible for planning, budget, process and production. Because imagination is the domain of experience design, there's every reason to take things to extremes when designing an experience centre. Designers all have their own aspirations and their imagination resonates with that of their clients. As a result, the ideas that are thought up are often too nice, too expensive, and too crazy. It's up to the project manager to keep the team on track, focused on an efficient, affordable project. Preparing and managing the production is also one of their core tasks.

Though that might make this team member sound like a bit of a stick in the mud, they have an important role to play in the creative process. The project manager must keep an eye on whether the team is on a promising path in terms of meeting both the wishes and requirements set by the client, thus directing the output of the entire team.

REFUSAL OF THE CALL

MEETING WITH TH

4.5 TO
STORYTELLING

The storyline is central to the development of a World of Wonder and is developed simultaneously to the spatial design. In this chapter, we'll discuss which steps go into making the story and see how the storyline is connected to the rest of the design process.

HOW THE STORY STARTS

In previous chapters, we described how the Big Idea stage involves drawing up the core purpose of a WoW, which then goes through the concept development stage to be turned into a visitor journey: the route the intended visitor will take through the scenes of the story. The following stage is concept design, which involves laying out the foundations of the design in terms of narrative, scenography and organisation.

The creative teams working on the project are kept together by a sort of two-component glue. The entire centre has to revolve around the *visitor*. After all, the starting point of experience design is that all designs must be made from their perspective. The second factor is the *story*. This relates to the objectives of a WoW: conveying a particular message in the most compelling way.

A clear storyline guides all creatives involved, including designers, copy-writers and audiovisual producers. It coordinates what they are working on.

This chapter is about developing such a storyline. Let's start looking at the different team roles and then at the glue itself: the Interpretation Strategy.

"Interpretation is an educational activity which aims to reveal meanings and relationships through the use of original objects, by first hand experience, and by illustrative media, rather than simply to communicate factual information."

– Freeman Tilden –

first sketch of a media fusion reactor

STORYTELLING ROLES

CONTENT SOURCING

This role involves identifying places, persons, objects and databases that could provide pieces of the story to be told. What is it about? Where are the experts to be found? Where can the objects be found and what are the highlights? These questions might look like preliminary research, but it is important during the whole process, because the story will be based on and proven by the sources at hand. In many cases, content sourcing will even continue after the centre is opened in order to keep its narrative up to date.

STORY DEVELOPMENT

This is about making the story suitable for experience design. The story developer uses the Interpretation Strategy to examine which aspects of the topic can be considered appealing for the target audiences. Based on these aspects, they can decide how to organise the narrative and what tone of voice to use. They will pick the appropriate narrative

techniques and decide which elements can be made interactive. It is also part of this role to determine what purpose the objects will serve and how they will be used in a meaningful way. In the later stages of the design process, story developers are in charge of safeguarding the consistency, intensity and rhythm of the storylines, all from the visitor's point of view, of course. This makes them a key supplier to and monitor of the design team.

CONTENT MANAGEMENT

The last role is all about managing the components and versions of the content, as well as sharing it with all people involved in the project. And there's a great number of people involved, because in addition to the creative tribes, the investors will also want to know whether everything is going according to plan. In the course of the design process, a flow of various versions of content components will arise and the value of managing this process carefully can hardly be understated.

CLIENTS AND CREATIVES

Many clients are inclined to conduct part of the story development themselves, because they have a lot of knowledge at their disposal, as well as the permission to use this knowledge.

This is also one of the reasons why it might not always be done by the client. For people inside the organisation, it can be difficult to tell a fresh story, without getting tangled up in complicated interests or drowning in details. An outsourced storyteller leads to new, objective and compact stories. Another reason is that in XD, story and design are so intertwined, that it leads to more effective processes and more exciting results when developed by the same team.

INTERPRETATION STRATEGY
FROM IDEA TO MESSAGE

Experience centres are built with the purpose of conveying ideas, which requires converting the synopsis into a core message. Based on an analysis of the characteristics of the intended visitor groups, you'll have to decide how to convey that message. The aim is to entice the target audience to pay attention to your subject and to do something with it. Communication experts will know this as a communication strategy, while in the world of experience design it's known as an Interpretation Strategy.

In the design stages that follow, this strategy is an important tool. The developers might agree on a scheme that they will follow to achieve the intended communication goals, such as: *"to get young people interested in the history of this old fort, we'll let them imagine that they're explorers. As they visit the fort, they'll make their own discoveries, digging a little deeper into the story with every new discovery."* Supplemented with other characteristics of the target audience (e.g. used to *new media and video games, short attention span, familiar with inquiry-based learning)*, this strategy specifies how to reach the target audience.

An Interpetation Strategy helps manage the volume and the level of the stories. While a WoW is being developed, a huge number of stories can emerge, thought up by people who know a great deal about the subject. They might have dedicated their entire career to the issue, or pour all their free time into it. These people are invaluable because they have an intimate relationship with the topic of the WoW. We like to call these people *treasure keepers.*

The core objective of interpretation is to convey that infatuation, which the public will, typically, not share at first. Treasure keepers often have trouble stepping into the shoes of someone looking into their field for the very first time and who is, therefore, unable to absorb everything at once. A good Interpretation Strategy serves as a guideline for these experts.

The chosen strategy is also useful when it comes to translating the story into scenes. It ensures that the WoW will be designed with the intended audience in mind. Tirpitz in West Jutland, Denmark, is a large museum targeted at visiting tourists, staffed by historians and archaeologists. Above his desk, the director of that museum hung an enormous placard emblazoned with the words 'we are not the visitor'. This is also an Interpretation Strategy, albeit a very succinct one. More advanced strategies include a study into the aspirations of these groups, allowing developers to see how they can best tailor the message to be as inspirational as possible.

In some cases, the Interpretation Strategy is supplemented with rules or limits that are agreed upon by all developers. One of these rules could be: 'limit all displays to 100 words' or 'attention over completeness'. This list lets all developers help each other to keep their word, which is of great importance for the coherence and thus the quality of the experience centre. In the list on this page, we suggest the applicable contents of such a plan.

INTERPRETATION STRATEGY CHECKLIST

√ **WHAT IS OUR MISSION?**
Backstory of initiating organization.

√ **WHAT IS THE CENTRE ABOUT?**
Synopsis of the story to be told including back story.

√ **WHO ARE OUR AUDIENCES?**
To be divided into primary and secondary audiences. Includes analysis.

√ **WHAT IS THE KEY MESSAGE?**
Insights & ideas to be conveyed.

√ **WHAT IS THE KEY EXPERIENCE?**
What adventure will people experience?

√ **WHAT IS THE KEY PURPOSE?**
Do you want to inspire, engage, educate, etc.?

√ **WHAT WILL PEOPLE LEARN & DO?**
What are the basic activities during the visit?

√ **WHAT ARE THE MUST-SEE ITEMS & STORIES?** Why are they essential?

√ **HOW WILL THE STORY BE TOLD?**
Key communication tactics.

THE INTERPRETATION STRATEGY ALSO INCLUDES

√ **DEFINITION OF QUALITIES.**
In terms of aesthetics, impact, materials, sustainability, etc.

√ **DOS & DON'TS** Agreements between all partners involved in the development process.

√ **DEFINITION OF SOURCES** Where can the stories be found or validated?

√ **WHO IS RESPONSIBLE FOR WHAT?** Demarcation and decision making during the process.

CONCEPT DESIGN
FROM MESSAGE TO NARRATIVE

The first design step consists of converting the synopsis into a series of ideas about how the message can be conveyed. It's up to the story developer to feed all others with highlights of the story and to check whether the message is in line with the Interpretation Strategy. A story scheme is made, the first linear layout of the content.

The general narrative that was set out in the visitor journey by means of a small number of sample scenes is now completed. This involves sequencing the most important moments that a visitor will go through. The different themes related to the main topic are developed in relation to each other in an overall structure.

In addition, this is the time to identify sources such as historical collections, photo and film archives, databases, safes full of source material and seasoned experts. All these elements are used to set up the exhibition, which means it's important to know where these sources are and whether they are accessible.

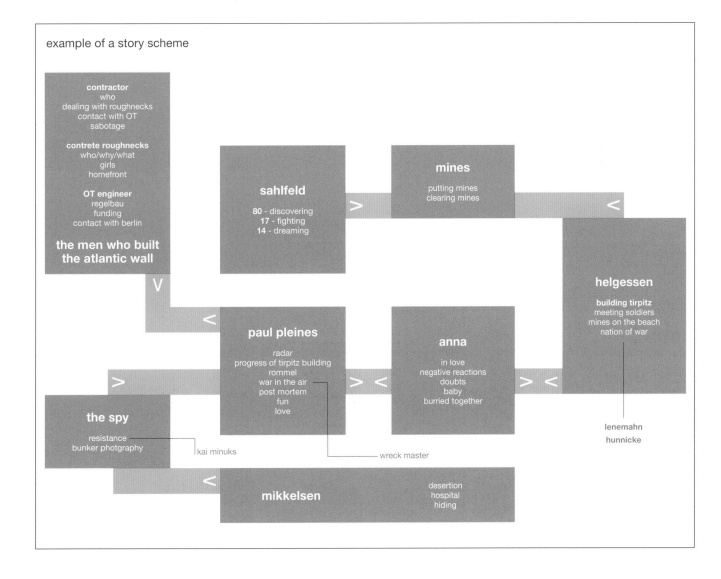

example of a story scheme

contractor
who
dealing with roughnecks
contact with OT
sabotage

contrete roughnecks
who/why/what
girls
homefront

OT engineer
regelbau
funding
contact with berlin

the men who built the atlantic wall

sahlfeld

80 - discovering
17 - fighting
14 - dreaming

mines

putting mines
clearing mines

helgessen

building tirpitz
meeting soldiers
mines on the beach
nation of war

paul pleines

radar
progress of tirpitz building
rommel
war in the air
post mortem
fun
love

anna

in love
negative reactions
doubts
baby
burried together

lenemahn

hunnicke

the spy

resistance
bunker photgraphy

kai minuks

wreck master

mikkelsen

desertion
hospital
hiding

DEVELOPED DESIGN
FROM NARRATIVE TO STORYLINES

At the next stage, which is known as developed design, all chapters of the journey are specified as the scenes of the adventure. The overall narrative is first divided into storylines for all themes involved and then into sub-stories. This involves positioning frame stories within the main storylines, maintaining a clear overview of the narrative as a whole. Is there a good balance between passive and active moments? Are we telling everything we want? Is there a good balance between action and rest? Will outsiders understand how everything is set in space and time? Is the storyline equally effective for all visitor groups? Asking these questions lets the developer create variety and draw up a complete topology of the experience centre.

It is now time to mine the sources that were mentioned before. This process is called *sourcing & clearing*. For each zone, the developers have to define which items are important, before finding, studying and preparing them, such as photo and video material, historical objects, technological components, or something else altogether. The better this process is performed, the more credible and authentic the story will be. (As in the courtroom, these are called exhibits). Mining and preparing source material is a task that is often underestimated, and organisations that aren't used to these processes can find it remarkably difficult. Even organisations that are familiar with it (such as museums) can find it hard to source their material. In some cases, they might have too many items or stories, leading to a problem of choice. There are various content management systems that can provide support in this matter by formally specifying the search through various templates, so that treasure keepers know exactly what they're being asked to find or come up with.

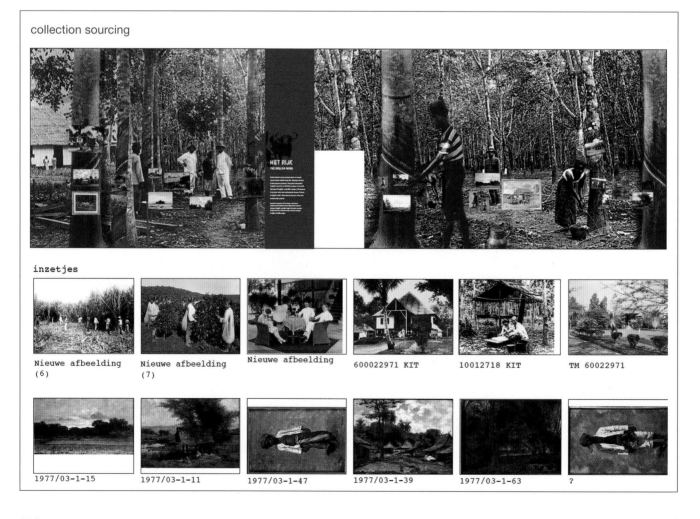

collection sourcing

inzetjes

Nieuwe afbeelding (6)

Nieuwe afbeelding (7)

Nieuwe afbeelding

600022971 KIT

10012718 KIT

TM 60022971

1977/03-1-15

1977/03-1-11

1977/03-1-47

1977/03-1-39

1977/03-1-63

?

FINAL DESIGN
FROM STORYLINES TO CONTENT DIAGRAM

The result of the last stage is a series of storylines intended for the various visitor groups, as well as a number of sub-stories featuring the objects. This is also known as the story scheme. All of this will be finalised in the final design stage, which serves to prepare the design for production.

All elements are now converted into a content diagram, which states exactly which content is conveyed where. This is also the time when scripts or storyboards for the audiovisual media are made.

Thanks to new media technologies, stories can now be told in a layered fashion, which is to say that visitors can determine how much information they want to take in. In the final design stage, the developers decide which content is assigned to which 'layer'. The same applies to multimedia scripts and information flow charts, that will ultimately guide the interaction. This phase concludes with a full overview and specification of all content in the entire experience centre.

content & collection diagram

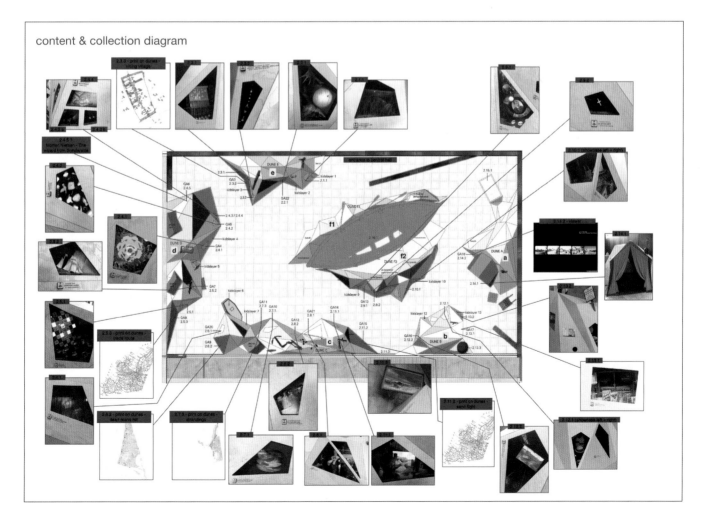

PRODUCTION
FROM DIAGRAM TO MEDIA CONTENT

While the exhibition is being built, the members of the storytelling team will work on producing actual text and audiovisual or multimedia content. The content diagrams are converted into copy, which will feature on walls, signs, panels, labels, or screens. The storyboards are converted into videos, and scripts are turned into voice-overs for media like audio devices, that typically provide more in-depth information. The matrix resulting from the final design phase serves as the blueprint for interactives, which display content as a game, or as information systems. Translations and special storylines for children are also produced at this point.

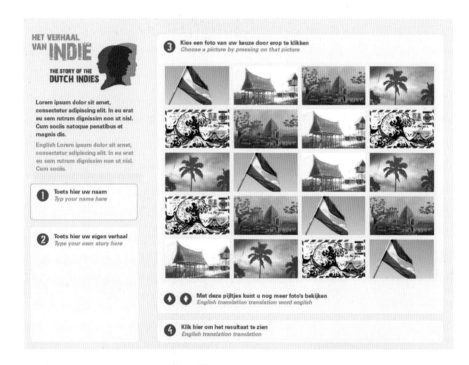

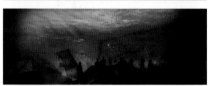

WHAT'S YOUR STATEMENT?

GO

So, this is the story of content. We hope to have shown that this is a task that has to be organised well. It is not a job you delegate to someone who is 'just' an expert on the issue, or who is not an expert at all, but an experienced traffic manager, for instance. It is complex, it requires different competencies and, when done properly, it is the backbone to a world full of wonder.

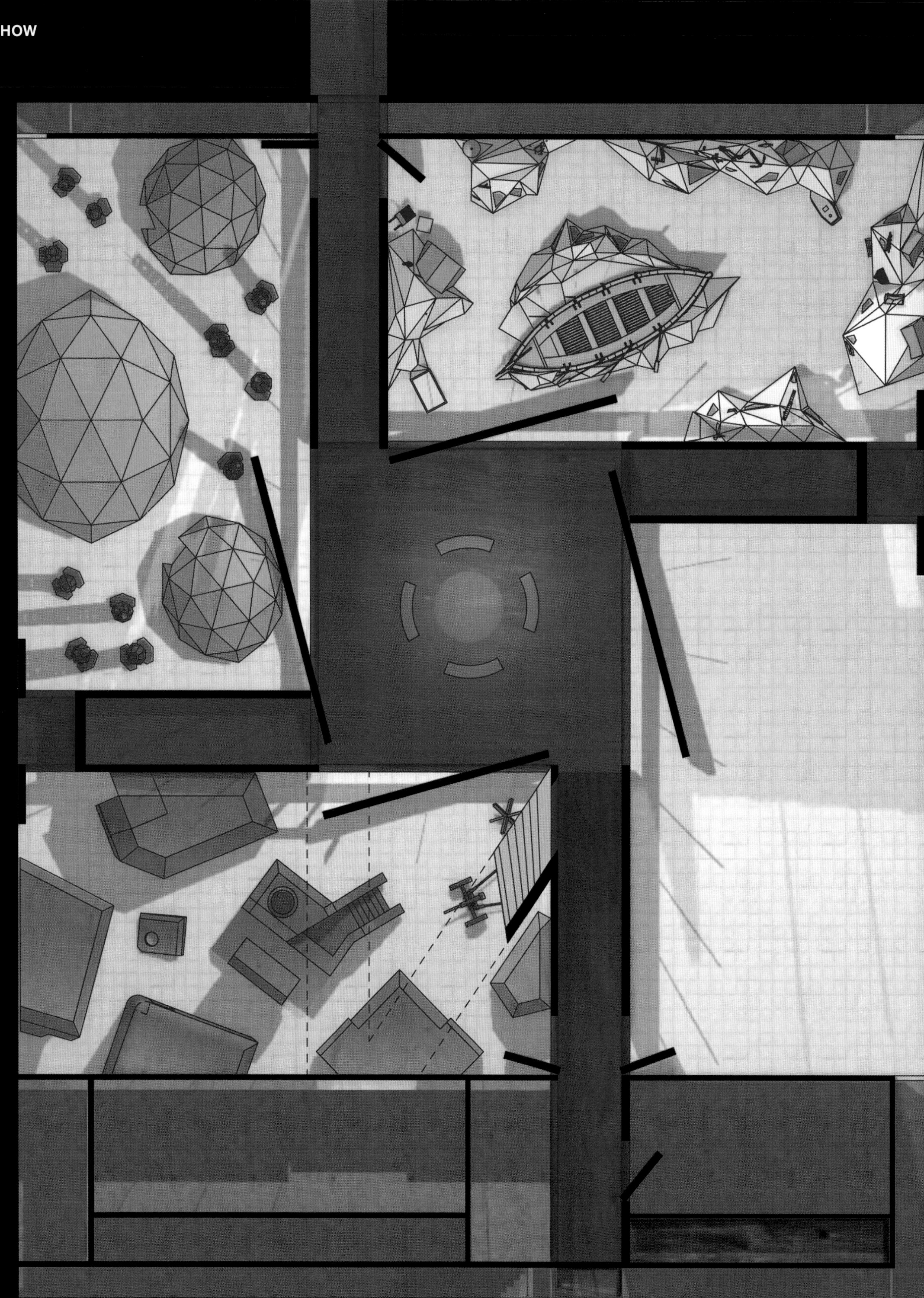

4 TO 6
DESIGN

Once the narrative is in place, the design has to specify how the storyworld will be laid out and materialised, which, as we saw earlier, is the domain of several disciplines. In this chapter, we will focus on the principles and steps of the design process. The trick of the trade is in arranging different creative powers to attain the best unified experience.

iD + 2D + 3D + 4D = XD

Even when it comes to the design track alone, XD is a multidisciplinary enterprise. In addition to all the ideas and stories involved, we're working with a lot of disciplines in many different dimensions: graphic design (2D), spatial design (3D), audiovisual and interaction design, light, sound and more.

Traditional exhibition design originated in museums, where conveying information and graphic plus spatial design always took centre stage. Experience design has its roots in the theme park & theatre world and as such it has always emphasised immersive and emotional quality. The link to audiovisual media, light and sound is almost self-evident. All these tools are used to add extra dynamics to the scenographic design.

Even this description, however, fails to mention another key dimension: the active influence of the visitors themselves. The main difference between experience design and movies, theatre and traditional museums is that the audience will be actively involved. That's why there's also a field called interaction design. Whereas it often comes down to designing individual exhibits that can be operated mechanically or by means of media in science centres, experience design sees interaction as wide-ranging opportunities for active contact between the visitor, the environment and the story.

All in all, experience design is a multidimensional field of expertise, so that you might say:
iD + 2D + 3D + 4D = XD

Now that we've looked at some of the design disciplines, it can be helpful to know what to expect during which phase of the process.

creating the Tirpitz museum

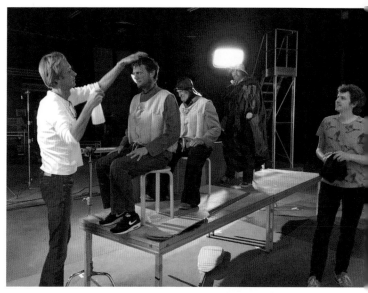

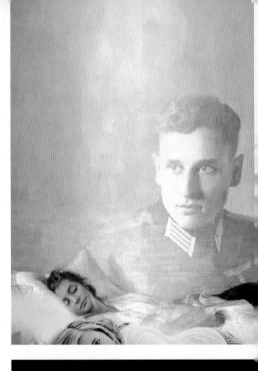

CONCEPT DEVELOPMENT
VISUALISING THE IDEA

This phase starts off with the Big Idea, which is often a document produced by a few people with a dream. The final product of this phase is a concept, master plan, vision document or some other presentation that manages to showcase the purpose of your WoW to (existing or potential) stakeholders. Although some of these presentations are and always will be digital, it's standard practice to create a hardy copy version known in the field as a bid book. Its main purpose is to garner support, raise funds or to explain the plans. It's as much a means of communication as it is the foundation on which the next design track will build.

Although the concept is full of images and sketches, this phase doesn't require any real design work yet. It's not uncommon to use reference images taken from other Worlds of Wonder that give an impression of what can

be expected later on. This is an effective method that helps you avoid addressing specific design matters too soon, so that you can focus on the essence of the concept. This stage is about getting everyone to buy into your vision, regardless of the details.

Having said that, visualisations are also a commonly used tool. They aren't designs yet either, but collages of images that highlight the core essence of your concept. Architects will often use high-definition renderings during this stage, but we've always found it more effective to leave a little more to the imagination. After all, we're looking to create a World of Wonder and spark the curiosity of future visitors.

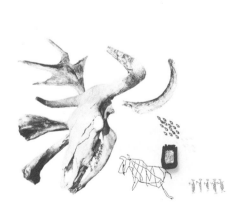

CONCEPT DESIGN
SETTING THE SCENE

The step from concept development to concept design is taken when the work continues within the specific parameters of the location, budget, requirements, goals, narrative and more. The first step often involves getting all these factors straight and translating them into workable design principles. This phase revolves around charting the main structure, styles and approaches for the World of Wonder. Building these foundations requires a lot of creative effort. Imagination is still key, engineering less so.

Once the framework is in place, sketching the main scenes of the journey is next. Visitor flow, experience and journey are all elaborated and translated until they fit within the spatial dimensions.

The overall scenes are then filled with preliminary shapes, objects and exhibits, just like a set designer uses props to create the right impression. At this point in time there's no need to know *all* story components and specific objects yet, although it's vital to get an idea of the type of content and objects you can expect.

In terms of which style to use for the design, sketched drafts will often do, as long as they demonstrate sufficient impact and coherence. This phase is finalised with a documented presentation that contains and unifies all principles, sketches, flows and impressions. Once it has been approved, this will be the fixed framework for the project.

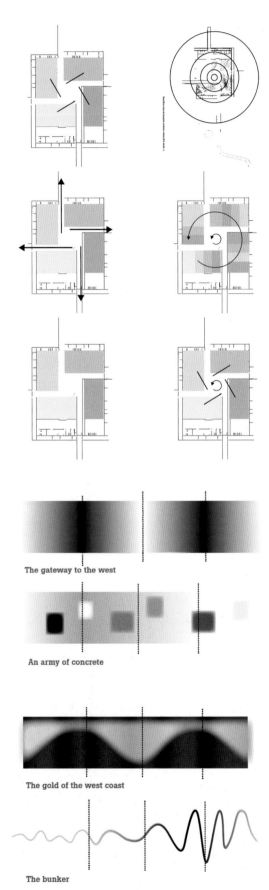

The gateway to the west

An army of concrete

The gold of the west coast

The bunker

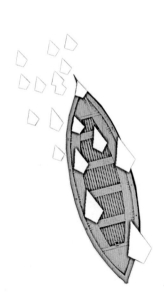

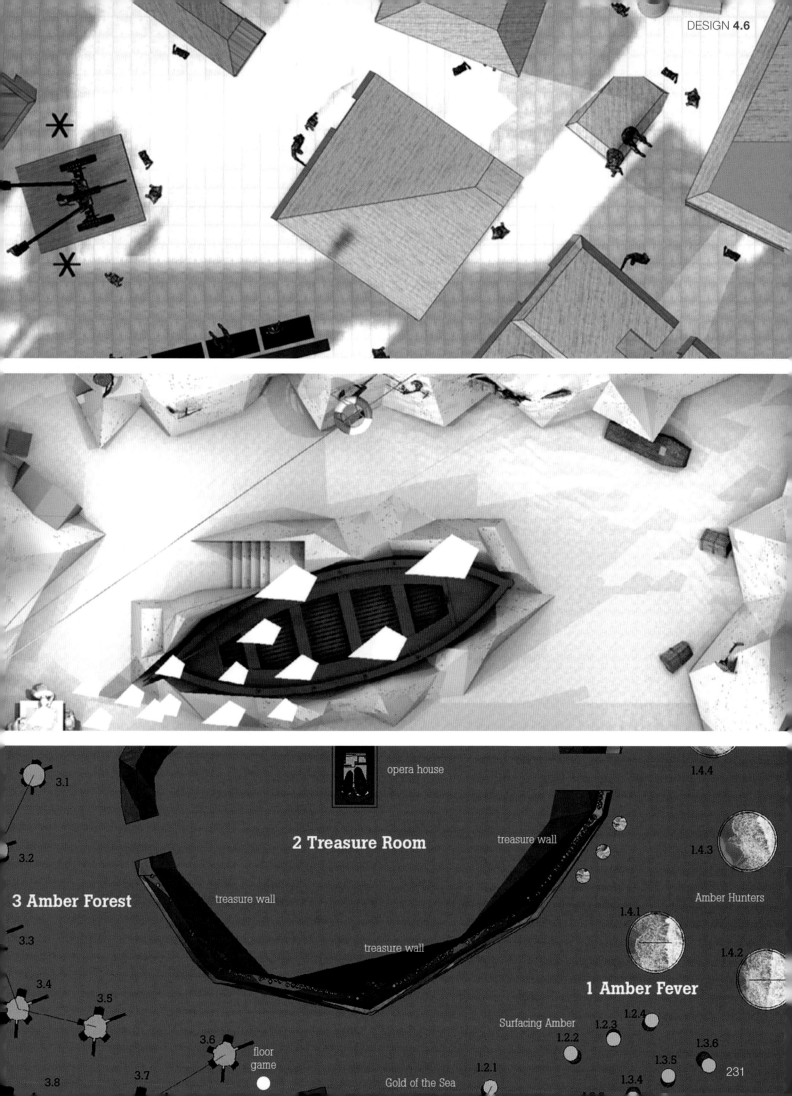

opera house

1.4.4

3.1

2 Treasure Room

treasure wall

1.4.3

3.2

3 Amber Forest

treasure wall

Amber Hunters

3.3

1.4.1

treasure wall

1.4.2

3.4

1 Amber Fever

3.5

3.6

Surfacing Amber

1.2.4

floor
game

1.2.2

1.2.3

1.3.6

3.7

1.2.1

1.3.5

3.8

1.3.4

Gold of the Sea

DEVELOPED DESIGN
DESIGNING THE EXPERIENCE

This is the main part of the design process, where principles will be applied to all components of the experience. The scenes are subdivided into smaller parts, before being cut into smaller elements still, each with their own signature. Within the developed design, each square foot of the World of Wonder has to be designed separately. This is when imagination will gradually start to be combined with engineering, which is the core part of all later stages.

During the developed design phase, variations on the design principles that were established earlier, allow for a varying and fitting family of experiences. This process involves determining how the individual parts of the story and components of the interior should be treated. Would it make more sense to make this an active or passive step and how much space should we allocate to it? How should we group the collection and where can we fit in text and audio? What is the most fitting style for the immersive experience we're looking for and how can it best be created? These are but a few of the myriad questions that will arise during this stage.

Attention must also be paid to the functionality of the interactive and technical components and the audiovisual content is given its own synopsis and custom style. The visual identity is implemented in designs for several applications, such as screen and label designs and the initial lighting designs and audio plans are made. The content and collection undergo preliminary selection, resulting in documents that give the designers more control over these items, as an ever more coherent whole starts to emerge. This phase ends with a complete overview of all the creative development for the WoW.

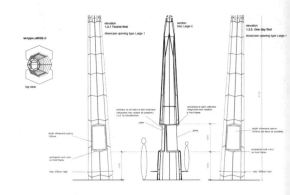

FINAL DESIGN
PREPARING FOR PRODUCTION

This brings us to the final design phase, which revolves around detailing and engineering the entire project, before preparing it for production. In practice, this phase often starts with smaller adjustments to the designs, based on the latest feedback. Whereas previous phases primarily revolved around the creative aspects of the project, this phase focuses on issues such as the practical construction, technical functionality, material quality, processing capacity and completeness of all components. Imagination clearly makes way for engineering.

The content of the story is now fixed, all objects have been selected and all elements meet the project requirements. All audiovisual content has been translated into storyboards and style briefings. Sample texts are written and tested. The lighting plan is finalised, both with regard to the light effects it intends to create and the fixtures that will be needed to do so, and detailed plans are made for audio production. As for 2D design, all visual and graphic elements must have been completed by the end of this phase and all spatial designs will

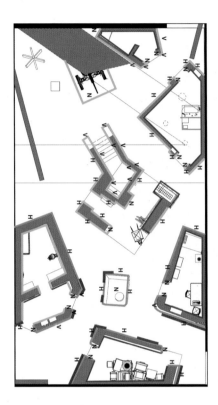

be specified, down to dimensions, materials, functions and construction. Numerous specialists are now involved in the project, varying from the fire department and hygiene specialists to experts who are tasked with linking the experience centre to education.

The final design contains briefings for all parties that will work on realising the experience, such as stage builders, programmers, filmmakers, lighting experts, stylists and hardware suppliers. There's often heavy traffic between the builders and designers, which revolves around transferring the project to the next phase and, primarily, finding solutions for design problems. This is also when the final, pinpoint adjustments are made to get all expenses, schedules and work sequences in line. The project manager will (literally) have to work overtime to make sure that what needs to be done is done correctly. This stage is completed when a final design document can be ratified containing all details, specifications and briefs for the production phase.

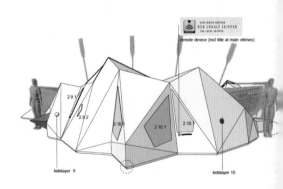

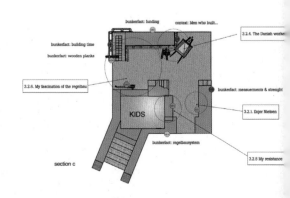

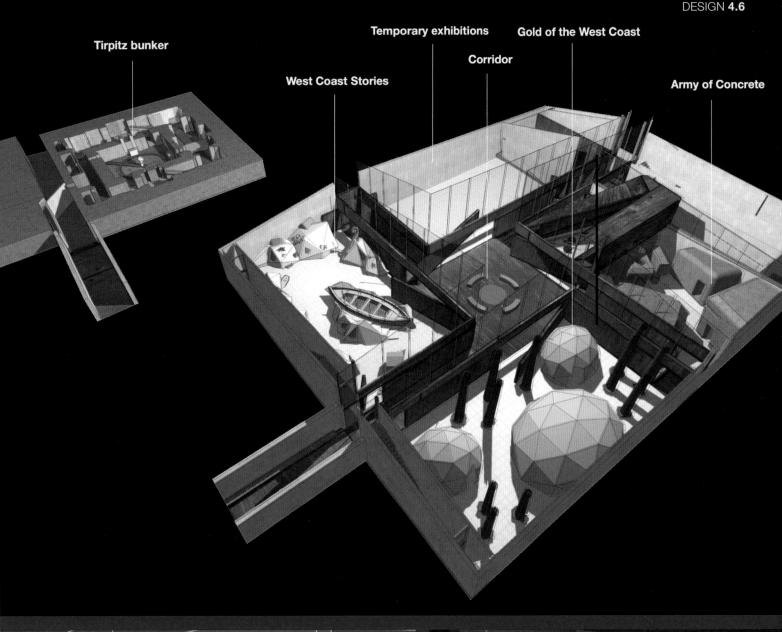

Tirpitz bunker

West Coast Stories

Temporary exhibitions

Corridor

Gold of the West Coast

Army of Concrete

PRODUCTION
CREATIVE DELIVERIES & QUALITY CONTROL

Although the design stages have now come to an end, there are still important roles reserved for the creative team during the production of the project. These vary from specific deliveries to quality control (the extensive role of production management will be described in the next chapter). The deliveries consist of so-called creative productions, with the following being the most common.

DESKTOP PUBLISHING (DTP)

First of all, there's DTP. Although all the graphic designs have been finalised, that doesn't mean that they're all ready for production. This is a common misunderstanding that stems from the difference between design and DTP. By the time that a graphic designer has finalised the complete design for 6 text sign templates, as well as the visual designs for 5 wall prints, for example, there's still a lot of work to be done. Your average design project, after all, could feature hundreds of text signs, which means that all 6 templates are yet to be applied (=DTP) to the 100 actual texts. As for the wall print, a full design isn't the same as a file for a 6x4 metre print sent to a specialised printing company, ready to be input into the machine. Preparing files such as these requires a lot of work, as the resolution of the design has to be scaled up if it's to look as brilliant in real life as it does on a screen. These DTP tasks are usually part of the production stage (and are charged to the production budget) because they concern physical deliverables.

COPYWRITING

The same applies to copywriting, which, in fact, boils down to text production. Writing text requires a lot of time and multiple corrections. The fact that the core of all content has now been specified in all sorts of clear and organised documents doesn't necessarily mean that the copy that the audience will ultimately read has already been written. Writing text is a skill in itself: content developers aren't always great copywriters. In some cases, the texts are written by experts (who are also in charge of content sourcing). This is mostly the case when working with informative or educational texts, as other types of texts are mainly written by an external copywriter (for more narrative or evocative copy).

AUDIOVISUAL AND MULTIMEDIA PRODUCTION

Production of audiovisual and multimedia content is next. This starts as soon as the storyboard is transformed into real shots and renderings with the right resolution (a crucial factor yet again, especially for large, immersive experience centres) and is converted into moving images. For AV, this phase involves editing existing material, shooting footage on location, animating stories or creating entire new, computer-generated worlds. For interaction design, production involves programming the interactive elements and applying the overall screen design to all the specific multimedia scenes on display.

ART DIRECTION

In addition to producing these creative deliverables, the main task of the design team during this phase pertains to quality control. This process is also known as art direction, but in view of the multidisciplinary nature of the design and the team behind it, we've found that quality control goes far beyond just artistic aspects in practice. The baton has now been passed to the builders and all plans have been specified and detailed properly, but it still remains necessary to constantly keep checking whether the more implicit ideas and expectations underlying the design are also implemented. It's impossible to formally specify every single aspect of an experience design, and builders simply focus on different things than designers do. As such, regular factory and on-site checks will be crucial for quality control. In the final delivery stage, the art director will usually make several laps through the project, followed by a pack of designers, managers with lists, suppliers with even longer lists and hopefully satisfied clients. The person in charge of quality control during this phase is typically not the most popular person on site. When it's time for drinks after the centre is opened, though, all the smiling faces are usually quick to forgive and forget.

A FINAL WORD

We hope that it's clear by now that good designs don't just revolve around creating great or even just fitting things, but that they're also a process of getting brilliant ideas to mesh with harsh reality. Some managers don't want issues like the budget and time limits to play a role in the design process, striving to give creativity full rein. Though it's an incredibly noble approach, it's not a good idea. If you focus entirely on the experience first and financial and other feasibility matters second, you'll usually end up with one or more elements that simply can't be made. You'll then have to adjust the design, which will give everyone the feeling that the final design isn't as good as the promise. It's better to make the budget part of the creative efforts: virtually all designers are capable of budgetary magic.

The next chapter will address how you can flesh this process out a little.

10,000 years of history turned into a 4D spectacle

4.7
COST
CONTROL

Experience design projects are often experimental in nature because they strive to communicate in a novel way or feature innovative media and technology. Regardless, they still require budget and time management. In what follows, we'll discuss a tried and tested management method, focused on cost and expectation management.

MANAGING EXPECTATIONS & UNCERTAINTY

Most experience centres arise from a Big Idea, as has been described in the previous chapters. They can be incredibly appealing and generate high expectations. Because this type of communication opens up a world of opportunities, it's easy to expect groundbreaking results in terms of profiling and reaching an audience. That expectation is justified, on the condition that the implementation of the plan is managed properly. The Big Idea is often devised at board level before being entrusted to third parties: an architect, a real estate agent or someone in the communications team. They are then commissioned to detail the concept and realise it. This requires that there isn't too great a discrepancy between their wishes and reality. Add to that the fact that experience design is a hyper-innovative sector that makes use of the latest design &media technologies, and that most people brought in to build an experience centre will be doing so for the first time. The most crucial factor in the whole process will soon emerge: uncertainty.

In the early design stages, this is a positive factor. Uncertainty implies a certain degree of freedom, which is necessary to allow several parties to contribute to the process, as a design agency and its client engage in playful dialogue. During earlier design phases, there's relatively little risk: design ideas can be tested and adjusted if necessary. In the worst-case scenario, you'll have to take your ideas back to the drawing board.

In later design phases, however, uncertainty should gradually decrease, before ultimately disappearing entirely. There'll come a point at which large sums of money have to be invested that can only be spent once. Many managers tend to combat uncertainty by requiring detailed specifications, using a method that used to be common in the building industry. By doing so, they strive to gain a complete overview of all costs and deliverables within the design process. After developing the over-view, a tender process is used to find contractors. This working method is expected to yield greater control and cost savings, partly due to the price-reducing mechanism inherent to the tender process: the winner is the 'Most Economically Advantageous' supplier.

Unfortunately, this form of project management doesn't always lead to the certainty you're looking for, nor to the best price. The reasons for this are as follows: you don't have a lot of insight into costs during the design phase, because there's no contractor involved to check your estimates. The client and designer constantly push each other upwards, as they keep making the project bigger and better. That's their shared ambition, after all. The bigger and better the project gets, though, the greater the risk that *all* the tenderers offer beyond the budget - and you won't find out until it's almost too late. That can be painful, because said board members will already have seen the plan a number of times and now expect nothing less than the original designs. They won't enjoy hearing that the final centre won't be quite as extraordinary as had been planned. Deletions belong to the earliest design stages and shouldn't be made the day before construction is due to start.

The main problem here is that the expertise of the construction specialists isn't used early enough in the process. They possess a wealth of knowledge with regard to materials and building techniques and if you're looking to build *top of the bill*, you really should make use of that knowledge. After the design has been finalised, there's little for suppliers/contractors to contribute to the plans for the simple reason that most decisions will already have been made, both with regard to inventive solutions and smart purchasing strategies.

ITERATIVE DESIGN & BUILD

There is much to be said for involving construction parties early on in the process and basing your selection on many more factors than on price alone. It's also wise to gradually reduce the degrees of freedom offered to the design and gradually increase purchasing certainties. But what about cost management? How do you properly delegate responsibilities? And how can you get the best results? We've had good experiences with a gradual transition method known as Iterative Design & Build (ID&B), which involves estimating and weighing ideas and costs in several iterations. These phases run parallel to the design phase and, in a way, they can even be considered part of it.

Let's look at the various phases:

BUDGET BREAKDOWN

During the Big Idea or concept phases, three things are important: the budget, the intended revenue and the promise. We'll now address each of these.

BUDGETING

Establishing a budget for an experience centre isn't all that easy to do. You'll be able to choose from several budget ranges that offer the functionality but lead to a completely different experience. You could compare it to picking a hotel room: you'll always have a bed and bathroom, but room prices can vary considerably. The difference is in the size of the room, the facilities at your disposal and the contents of the minibar. The same goes for experience centres: you can tell a story even with modest means. You might say that all you really need is a gifted storyteller. However, you could also choose to go all out in terms of architecture and media technology. The story might be the same, but the experience will be completely different. Which option to choose depends mainly on *representation*: how do you

want to come across, what do you consider appropriate for your organisation and for the person visiting the experience centre?

There are two ways to decide, both of which are more or less like Booking.com. The first is to simply compare the options. Find a number of public destinations that you'd like to resemble in terms of facilities and ask what they cost (while you're at it, ask about their annual operational costs as well, see the following chapter). The second way is to look into standard rates per square meter, which most design agencies will be able to give you. These standard rates include all expenses per square meter, including design, construction and installation costs. You can then determine a rough budget for your experience centre by multiplying the intended square footage of your centre with the standard rate. Agencies that are capable of working at several budget levels will also be able to show you reference images with different levels of execution

corresponding to the rates. You'll literally be able to see what you can expect with your budget: just like on Booking.com.

On the other side of the equation, you'll find the revenues generated by an experience centre. This may be cold hard cash, the result of ticket sales and sponsorships/subsidies, but can also constitute indirect returns, such as reputation, cultural value, staff satisfaction, or support for your plans. It's wise to quantify these factors, as this will let you see whether the operation is on track and whether you're getting sufficient return on investment. Earlier on, we described the change you manage to effect in your visitor, or the transformation in knowledge, attitude or behaviour you manage to set in motion, as an immaterial goal of an experience centre. All of this can be quantified.

In the next chapter, we'll focus on revenue.

CONCEPT DESIGN
THE ESTIMATED ITEM LIST

As we described in the previous chapter, the concept development phase involves fitting the Big Idea into the available space and thinking about how the story can be conveyed to visitors. This leads to a list of ideas for exhibits, videos, sets, activities, or whatever element you'd like. It's up to the project manager to keep this list up to date.

This list is supplemented with a demarcation statement, a list of architectural/engineering matters that must be included either in the construction budget or the exhibition budget, such as floors, lighting, ceiling finishes and infrastructure. The expenses involved can be significant, so it can be useful to know which budget they'll come

out of in advance. During this phase, you'll be able to say something about whether the promise devised in the Big Idea is at all realistic, given the net budget (sometimes there are so many project requirements that there's hardly any funds left for the experience itself. If that's the case, it's best that you find out early on).

The project manager then lists all expenses for the ideas included in the concept design, the adjustments that have to be made to the building and all other elements, culminating in a total budget. During this phase, experienced project managers will be able to estimate the total costs with an accuracy of about 15%.

DEVELOPED DESIGN
CALCULATIONS

In the preliminary or developed design phase, the ideas are worked out in greater detail and contractors are brought into the process to check your expense estimates. They submit their quotations to the project manager, who draws up a revised list based on actual costs, rather than an estimation. These quotations will often exceed the budget, simply because the designers came up with more ideas than are actually possible. This is an inherent part of a creative process and isn't much of a problem at all, as long as you're still at the beginning of the developed design phase. Everything is still possible. The designers now start working with the contractors to adjust their designs and make them fit the budget. The value of involving suppliers at an early stage will now become apparent, as the suppliers will also contribute to finding a solution. They might suggest merging certain items, building them differently, or using a smarter purchasing strategy. The client is also involved in the process, deciding which parts are essential and which items can be dropped. The experience director then checks whether the promise established in the initial plan will survive after these changes are made, based on the Interpretation Strategy. All parties involved want to optimise results, so everyone will automatically strive to make the most out of the available budget. The developed design phase results in an item list that looks like the list generated in the concept design phase, but now with an accuracy that is closer to 10%.

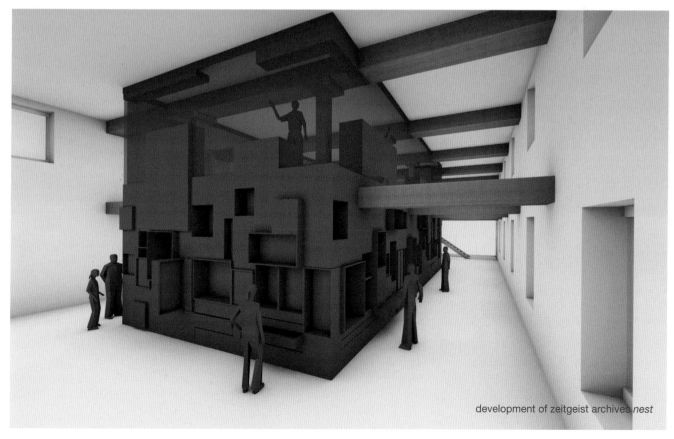

development of zeitgeist archives *nest*

FINAL DESIGN
VALUE ENGINEERING AND ORDERS

During the final design phase, the design is made ready to be sent over to the construction parties, as samples are made for materialisation, construction and graphic design. This phase focuses on the material qualities of the experience. Prototypes can also be made in earlier design phases, but they shouldn't be postponed beyond this phase, as you still want to be able to adjust your design based on the test results. In some cases, future visitors are invited to be present during the tests, allowing for early visitor testing as well. In this stage, the client will be asked to choose between various materials and facilities. The budget becomes increasingly accurate, *but the budget determined in the very first phase is still considered the final total.* Because all parties involved are familiar with this budget, they can keep making adjustments until their deliveries fit the budget: value engineering. Not a cent has been spent on production yet, however, this stage is all about planning & pre-production. Combining a budget that gradually becomes more accurate with delayed orders allows the client to stay in control, much more so than with a traditional tender method. Don't forget that you wouldn't have any information about pricing until after this phase in a traditional tender! A final version of the item list is generated, consisting of the negotiated quotations submitted by suppliers. Because they are quotations, this should, in theory, be a 100% accurate budge in theory, adding up to the total budget specified earlier. Naturally, it's always a good idea to keep a 5-10% margin in mind. It is now time to start realising the design with reliable cost overviews and clear, detailed assignments.

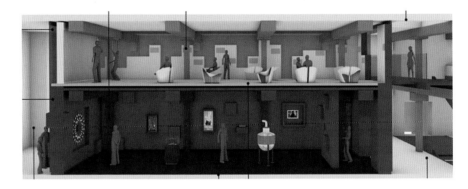

PRODUCTION
PRODUCTION & COST MANAGEMENT

During the construction phase, the parties in charge of building the exhibition will share their drawings with the designer for a final check. The architect, experience designer and contractor will meet to coordinate the various processes and the client will check how the exhibition is progressing via Factory Acceptance Tests (FAT). This also applies to software, such as films, games and interactives. In theory, no more changes should be made to the budget at this point, as all suppliers should be expected to comply with their quotations. In practice, however, small expenses might arise, due to new, additional wishes or aspects that had previously been overlooked. It can therefore be a smart idea to reserve part of the budget for unforeseen changes, made available only to the client and the project manager, who must consult with each other if they wish to make use of the budget (if either party is given free rein, this budget will soon be depleted). The construction phase ends with an on-site delivery, concluding with all contractors, the project manager and the experience or art director walking through the centre. During this so-called Site Acceptance Test (SAT),

a final snag list is drawn up, including all matters that still have to be completed before the delivery can be accepted. This, too, is in the interest of all parties involved, so it generally happens quickly. If all outstanding deliverables were already specified in the quotations, the snag list shouldn't have any consequences for the budget. And that's how you complete a project on budget.

CONTRACTING

A good project is delivered on time and on budget and meets all quality requirements. Seasoned professionals will know, though, that guaranteeing two out of three is easy, but managing all three is extremely difficult. The iterative approach is your best bet to ensure that none of the above items dominates the others, because they are continuously calibrated throughout the project.

The method described above has clear advantages: the available budget is fixed during all phases. In the event that the estimates are exceeded, the design is adjusted rather than the budget, unless the client explicitly chooses to do so. Because of the gradual specification, the client will have access to the planned expenditures, allowing them to take decisions at every step. The item lists are completely transparent: the client will never have to deal with surprises or irreversible facts. Finally, this method also gives the creative process the space it needs to be the most effective (prototyping), while motivating all contributors to make the most of the available budget by relying on their own expertise.

Naturally, this method has its own limitations and comes with certain conditions. The first precondition is that construction parties be brought in at an early stage, making it clear that you're interested in a partner, not someone trying to sell you something. After all, you don't want suppliers to paint an overly positive picture (which can happen in sales situations), but to remain realistic. This also means that the contractors must be able to rely on the fact that they will ultimately supply what they're being asked to.

At this point, suppliers can't be selected based on pricing, because the designs won't be specific enough to make any meaningful comparisons. If you start a tender process in this stage, suppliers will compete on budget range & synergy, rather than price optimisation. The budget range, however, should be determined by the client, not by the supplier. That is why this method doesn't rely on tenders when selecting partners, but on reputation and trust.

Procurement professionals may have their doubts about contracting third parties at such an early stage, because it seems to remove any incentives for competitive pricing. Who will make sure that the suppliers quote competitive prices when they no longer have to compete with others? A solution may be to bring in an external calculation agency to draw up the iterations, or to have the design agency do this (or both). In both cases, the construction party won't be involved in the process yet, which means their expert knowledge cannot yet be used.

A second precondition is that the promise and delivery be delegated to the same party. Everyone will have come across a dramatic renovation where various suppliers held others accountable for any holes in the budget or the floors. These situations are usually the result of poor coordination or demarcation. A typical feature of these surprises is that they often arise during the installation process. By the time you make it to this phase, there's hardly any wiggle room to eliminate potential problems, which is a surefire recipe for stress.

We already outlined part of the solution above: make sure that any holes in the budget become visible in the concept or developed design at the latest. During those phases, there's still some breathing room. A second solution is to have the experience design agency implement it as well. They know the market well and are also responsible for the communicative effectiveness of the exhibition. If the same party is also in charge of delivering the centre, they can be held accountable for the communicative strength of the experience centre and the quality of the delivery. Combining these two factors will guarantee good results. Procurement processes don't always allow for this. However, the advantages of this method also benefit the procurer, so having a good conversation about this issue could well be worth your while. All in all, the procurement process for experience centres is often slightly different than for other projects.

These measures let you control uncertainty, which is simultaneously the most creative and most limiting factor in a construction process. Of course, multiple roads lead to Rome: there's no such thing as the perfect construction process (yet). Ours is an innovative field that's rich in opportunities to make ever more beautiful experience centres.

THE STEPS OF ITERATIVE DESIGN & BUILD

The Iterative Design & Build (ID&B) method combines budget certainty with creative freedom, making the most of the expertise of everyone involved.

STEP 1
PREPARATION & BRIEF

The client draws up a demarcation list in cooperation with the architect and experience designer. This list can be used as a basis for a budgeted general list of deliverables for the exhibit.

STEP 2
CONCEPT DESIGN

The experience designer translates the assignment into a number of exhibition ideas. These ideas are budgeted and added to an item list. The total costs equal the budget established in step 1.

STEP 3
DEVELOPED DESIGN

As soon as the first ideas have been conceived and budgeted, one or more contractors are involved in the process. They are introduced to the item list and total budget and commit to sticking to the budget. The total costs are equal to the budget established in step 1, unless the client makes adjustments to the available budget.

STEP 4
FINAL DESIGN

The experience director specifies the idea and the construction party calculates construction & installation costs. If the total costs of the items exceed the total budget, a) items are deleted, b) items are made cheaper, or c) the budget is increased. The client has the final vote in this matter.

STEP 5
CONSTRUCTION AND INSTALLATION

At the end of the technical design phase, the definitive item list is drawn up, along with corresponding quality requirements. The items on the list are then built and installed. Because the client, design agency and builder(s) have all been familiar with the item list and total budget for some time, no one will have to deal with any surprises at this point. Because everyone involved wants to achieve the best possible result, they'll all make every effort to come up with solutions that fit the budget, with each party relying on their own knowledge and expertise. Thanks to the transparency of the budgeting process, the client will have more control over the costs incurred.

CONCEPT DEVELOPMENT	CONCEPT DESIGN		DEVELOPED DESIGN		FINAL DESIGN		PRODUCTION	
WISH LIST WoW	ITEM A	€€	ITEM A1	€€	ITEM A2	€€	ITEM A3	€€
	ITEM B	€€	ITEM B1	€€	ITEM B2	€€	ITEM B3	€€
	ITEM C	€€	ITEM C1	€€	ITEM C2	€€	ITEM C3	€€
	ITEM D	€€	ITEM D1	€€	ITEM D2	€€	ITEM D3	€€
	ITEM E	€€	ITEM E1	€€	ITEM E2	€€	ITEM E3	€€
	ITEM F	€€	ITEM F1	€€	ITEM F2	€€	ITEM F3	€€
	......	......	......	......	......	......	......	......
DEMARCATION								
WISH LIST BUILDING	ITEM U	€€	ITEM U1	€€	ITEM U2	€€	ITEM U3	€€
	ITEM V	€€	ITEM V1	€€	ITEM V2	€€	ITEM V3	€€
	ITEM W	€€	ITEM W1	€€	ITEM W2	€€	ITEM W3	€€
	ITEM X	€€	ITEM X1	€€	ITEM X2	€€	ITEM X3	€€
	ITEM Y	€€	ITEM Y1	€€	ITEM Y2	€€	ITEM Y3	€€
	ITEM Z	€€	ITEM Z1	€€	ITEM Z2	€€	ITEM Z3	€€
	......	......	......	......	......	......	......	......
+	€€€	=	€€€	=	€€€	=	€€€	= €€€
BUDGET	ESTIMATION (+/- 15%)		CALCULATION (+/- 10%)		ORDERS (+/- 5%)		CONTINGENCIES (+/- 0%)	

OPERATION

In the final chapter, we'll discuss a number of points of interest that are important when setting up an operational plan. We'll share a combination of content-related, contractual and organisational points that are crucial to consider when preparing for the operational phase. If you don't take these issues to heart, running an experience centre can be more difficult than developing it.

OPENING YOUR DOORS

The opening of an experience centre is a transition moment in itself. The weeks and days leading up to the big moment are typically rather busy: no matter how well a project is planned, in some mysterious way there's always a great amount of work to be done in the final weeks. During the opening, everyone is happy and excited as all guests remark on the beauty of the end result. Then Tuesday morning comes around (most experience centres are closed on Mondays) and the first real visitors appear. They're different from the guests who were invited to attend the opening because these visitors have come to the centre of their own accord. Maybe they planned their visit long ago, or maybe they just happened to be in the area. No matter what, they'll be doing something very special: they are going to use the place. You can be sure that they won't do so on your terms, but in their own way. *The centre has become theirs.* That doesn't matter, as long as everything works. This chapter addresses how you can optimise the day-to-day operations of a World of Wonder and keep it running in the long term.

When it comes to operations, it's best to see a visitor centre as a little company of its own, with its own staff, its own operating budget and its own budget for growth and development. This is a self-evident step for organisations that are familiar with hosting visitors, such as museums, but organisations with a different core business tend to underestimate it. Creating a public destination will generate a constant flow of new visitors to your organisation, which can give a great boost, if you organise it well.

OPERATIONAL MANAGEMENT

We choose three key issues
for preparing to run your centre:
marketing, visitor management
and the operating budget.

MARKETING

Marketing revolves around attracting
the right audience to your centre,
which is something you'll have to
start doing long before it opens.
You'll have to translate the 'Invitation'
into a plan on how to draw visitors
(see 1.6), which includes elements
such as a website, launch event,
press moment, appropriate ticket
prices and an online booking system.
Social media are currently a decisive
factor as to how a new destination
is perceived, so make sure to have
a good social media strategy in
place. It's even more important than
a slick new website. Obviously,
marketing an experience centre
means conquering an uninhabited
island in people's schedules, which
is not the same as marketing the
product your organisation is used to
promoting. This is even the case if
your organisation is used to selling
exhibitions. The spectacular nature of
a World of Wonder calls for a different,
more imaginative approach.

VISITOR MANAGEMENT

Decide well in advance whether
you want to allow people to navigate the centre independently or
whether you want them to be guided.
This decision should be incorporated
into the design and will determine
how many guides you'll need and/or
how many people you can host in
one day. More generally, you'll need
an accurate estimate of how many
staff members you'll need to run the
place in an efficient way. All too often,
finalising the project takes centre
stage and people forget that they'll
need a team that's ready to take
over from the internal developers.
These people then tend to 'hang
around' and take this task upon
themselves, but running a centre
doesn't necessarily require the
same skills as developing one.
Besides, it's hardly a part-time job.
Keeping up with bookings, receiving
visitors, some of whom are VIPS,
detecting and remedying teething
problems, organising all services in
and around the centre and ensuring
that it meshes well with the rest of
the organisation are all major tasks
that require undivided attention.
Understaffed centres won't do
justice to the investments, which is
a particular shame at a time when
PR is at an all-time high. Bigger
design agencies will be capable of
advising you about optimal staffing
levels and some agencies will even
provide turnkey visitor centres with
a team in place.

OPERATING BUDGET

This brings us to the operating
budget, the third factor that must
never be forgotten when founding
an experience centre. Staffing is
the largest expense here, but rent,
marketing, service & maintenance,
replacement investments and
depreciation must also be taken
into consideration, with the latter in
particular being just as important as it
is underestimated. A World of Wonder
has a limited lifespan, especially in
view of the rapid developments
in the field of media technology.
The interior of a WoW will typically
remain current for about 10 years,
but it can easily be less in some
cases. Many organisations tend to
adopt a laissez faire attitude and
when the time comes to renovate
a centre, they go looking for funding
for the next release. However, starting
to account for depreciation early
on in the process is a very smart
move. Although it depends on which
administrative system an organisation
has in place, this process can be used
to generate investments for the next
version somewhere in the future.
In any case, it's always important
to have a properly dimensioned
operating budget. There are enough
notorious examples of great visitor
centres that had to shut down
prematurely. The losses in those
cases are enormous, because
investments made in a WoW are
difficult to convert: there is no market
for second hand WoWs.

IMMEDIATELY AFTER OPENING
SNAG LISTS

Immediately after your place opens, there are three types of improvement that you'll have to tackle to provide your audience with an optimal service.

TECHNICALITIES

The first type of improvement is technical in nature and involves ensuring that your show control systems and interfaces are stable and functional. This is a relatively easy point, because it's typically covered by the warranties provided by suppliers. The stability of these systems has improved significantly over the past decade, which is a good thing, as there's hardly anything more annoying than 'out of order' signs on exhibits that should have been operational. The points for improvement are added to the snag list and it's in everyone's interest that these points be addressed as quickly as possible, which is why it generally doesn't take too long to solve these issues.

LOGISTICS

The second type of improvement relates to logistics and involves visitor behaviour through the experience and staff training. You can never completely predict visitor flows and your staff members still have to get to know the visitors they'll be dealing with. There may be certain bottlenecks in the adventure or gaps in the flow of visitors due to sub-optimal opening hours, complicated routing or the wrong access conditions, which includes pricing. To address these issues you'll have to train your staff and tweak the programme. In virtually all cases, it doesn't amount to much more than smoothing out the wrinkles and you'll achieve an optimal situation after a few weeks or months.

OWNERSHIP

The third area for improvement involves the point we opened this chapter with: having the visitors take ownership of the WoW. People will use the centre in their own way, which means they might have other needs than you had anticipated. You might, for example, have introduced a certain component to evoke wonder, but find that it works so well that your visitors also want answers to the questions that arise. In those cases, it's advisable to find a way to provide these answers. In other cases, children might struggle to focus on a particular component because it's too easy or too complicated, which means the functionality will have to be adjusted. For these purposes, updates are required to significantly improve the experience, or rather the way it's processed.

OPERATING PERIOD
SERVICE AND MAINTENANCE

After all the snag lists have been completed and the staff has learnt how to provide visitors with an optimal experience, it's time to optimise all the operational processes of the visitor centre. One of the key components is service & maintenance, as the warranty periods for the deliveries lapse into service contracts.

The vast majority of WoWs consist of multimedia installations with a rather complex infrastructure. It's important that they work with as little downtime as possible, but the information technology used often isn't the same as the technology used by the hosting organisation. Most centres we know of run on autonomous IT networks.

With regard to service and maintenance, most visitor centres are hosted based on a three-ring model:

THE FIRST RING consists of on-site maintenance employees, or the internal staff members. They will fix minor issues and take care of daily maintenance

---

THE SECOND RING consists of 24/7 remote control by specialised service organisations. They are capable of controlling the entire system remotely and can fix virtually all issues online.

THE THIRD RING consists of regular maintenance, including parts of the centre's decor and mechanical components, which can't be done remotely.

These three services will be combined in an SLA, which also covers spare parts (make sure to determine whether these spare parts belong to the delivery or operation phase very early on; a typical demarcation issue that's often overlooked). This system will allow you to preempt outages, keeping the centre open to the public at all times. Other maintenance-related issues such as cleaning, staff scheduling and insurances aren't all that different in other parts of an organisation, which is why we won't discuss them here.

FUTURE
A NEW BEGINNING

Now that the place is up and running, it is good to realise that you haven't just started an experience centre, but an expertise centre as well. How many places focus on the same subject that you do? You can join these to form a network of expertise with ever increasing knowledge about how to convey the subject to your intended audience. The fact that your audience becomes more knowledgeable about your subject will feed back on itself. After founding a historical, scientific or brand centre, you'll become a cultural attractor, thus boosting your story or subject. You'll be approached by new parties who want to work with you in all sorts of different partnerships. Operating a World of Wonder revolves around expanding that position and thus providing added value to society.

In addition, a public environment will give a strong boost to the organisation that developed it. This is evident for museums, as it is the very core activity of the organisation behind the centre. For many organisations that have not had this public function before, however, matters are different. They have become an 'open house' for the entire world, which will affect all employees, ranging from the board to receptionists. Becoming a destination will cause you to evaluate what your organisation and your people stand for, which often strengthens internal bonds and makes it easier to establish new external relationships. You can use this for the future development of your WoW by having staff members author new components, train new employees in the centre or organise outreach projects with educational institutions.

All in all, the possibilities are endless, both during development and operation. A newly opened experience centre is the result of a long process and the beginning of a new one.

257

5

NOW

NOW, IT'S UP TO YOU

So here we are, having described how a World of Wonder is developed from the very first idea to its operation. We also discussed the rapid growth of this wonderful industry, set against a background of world-wide trends, sharing the passions and purposes involved.

Now it's up to you. If you've read this book, we're almost sure that you take a very close interest in this field. That's worthy of congratulations. It's the greatest job there is: visualising exciting ideas, telling remarkable stories and designing transformative adventures. Who wouldn't want to do this? We believe the world could use many more places that provide inspiration to a large audience. So, here's a call to all clients, visionaries, pioneers and creatives: more experiences for curious people, more WoW!

We wish you lots of inspiration.

Stan & Erik

KEYWORD INDEX

CREDITS

PHOTOGRAPHERS

MB	Mike Bink
EB	Erik Bär
TI	Tinker Imagineers
FP	Fred Prak

cover	Author photo by Maarten Willemstein

All images are part of projects designed by Tinker Imagineers, except otherwise indicated.

2–3
- Dalí Theatre-Museum, *creator* artist Salvador Dalí, Figueres, Spain, EB

6
- Stonehenge, Amesbury, United Kingdom, EB
- La Scarzuola, *creator* architect Tomasso Buzzi, Montegabbione, Italy, EB
- Holocaust Memorial, *creator* architect Peter Eisenman, Berlin, Germany, EB
- Santa Maria in Trastevere, Rome, Italy, EB
- Pompeii, Italy, EB

8–9
- VHG pavilion, Floriade, Almere, TI
- The American Indian, The New Church, Amsterdam, the Netherlands, EB
- The Magic of the Bubble, Science Centre NEMO, Amsterdam, the Netherlands, FP
- Continium, Continium Kerkrade, the Netherlands, TI
- Tinkerish, Utrecht, the Netherlands, Jasper Lensselink
- Concept visual, Liberty Museum, Nijmegen, the Netherlands, TI

10–11
- Caves of Lascaux, Lascaux International Centre for Cave Art, Montignac, France, EB

14
- City of the Netherlands, Netherlands Architecture Institute, Rotterdam, MB

17
- Concept image, TI

18
- Concept image, TI
- Concept image, TI
- Museum Spakenburg, the Netherlands, EB
- Sant'Ignazio di Loyola, Rome, Italy, EB

20–25
- Nest, Vevey, Switzerland, MB

26
- Jewish Museum, *creator* architect Daniel Libeskind, Berlin, Germany, EB

29
- Concept visual for the Liberty Museum, Nijmegen, the Netherlands, TI

30
- Nest, Vevey, Switzerland, TI
- Concept visual for the World of Silver, Dutch Silver Museum, Schoonhoven, the Netherlands, TI
- Lustrum of the University of Utrecht, the Netherlands, FP
- The Sea Voyage, National Maritime Museum, Amsterdam, the Netherlands, MB

32
- Heineken Experience, Amsterdam, The Netherlands, MB

34
- Earthwalk, Rabobank, Floriade 2012, Almere, the Netherlands, MB

36
- Concept image, TI

CREDITS

38–39
- Global mind, Science Centre NEMO, TI
- Robot image, TI

40
- A.I. stand, 350 year anniversary, University of Utrecht,
  the Netherlands, source unknown
- Logo of Firma Luchtkasteel, TI

41
- Living Technology, Children's theatre,
  Science Centre NEMO, FP

43
- Book cover of The Tree of Knowledge: The Biological Roots
  of Human Understanding by Humberto Maturana and
  Francisco Varela, Shambhala publications, 1992

44
- A Tinker at work, source unknown
- Nikola Tesla, source unknown
- Summer exhibition 'Powers of Ten', Science Centre NEMO, FP

45
- Alcoa advertisement, Time Magazine 16-02-1942
- Walt Disney in front of the E.P.C.O.T blueprint in 1966,
  Walt Disney Enterprises
- Tinker imagineers creative studio, TI

46–47
- Tinker imagineers creative studio, TI

48
- Tinker imagineers creative studio, Maarten Willemstein

49
- Tinker imagineers creative studio, MB, photo bottom left
  by Maarten Willemstein

50
- Anatomical Theatre, Rijksmuseum Boerhaave,
  Leiden, the Netherlands, MB

53
- Landgoed Beeckestijn, Velsen-Zuid, the Netherlands, MB
- Taste Station, Floriade, Almere, the Netherlands, MB
- TU Delft Science Centre, the Netherlands, MB
- Summer exhibition 'Chemistry by the Sea',
  Science Centre NEMO, FP

56
- Professor Splash, Maritime Museum,
  Rotterdam, the Netherlands, MB
- Liberation Route Europe, MB

57
- Geert Groote House, Deventer, the Netherlands, MB
- Radio Darfur, Netherlands Refugee Foundation, FP

58–59
- Taste Station, the Netherlands, MB

60
- Nest, Vevey, Switzerland, EB

62
- Concept visual for the Children's Gallery, Maritime Museum,
  London, United Kingdom, TI
- Concept visual for the Climate House, Oslo, Norway, TI
- Concept visual for the National Geographic Campus,
  Washington D.C., USA, TI

63
- Concept visual for the Van Gogh expo, TI
- Concept visual for the Artis Museum, TI
- Concept visual for the National Geographic Campus,
  Washington D.C., USA, TI

66
- World Soil museum, Wageningen University and Research
  Centre, the Netherlands, MB

67
- The Cannenburch Castle, Vaassen, the Netherlands, MB
- Earthwalk, Rabobank, Floriade 2012,
  Almere, the Netherlands, MB

68–69
- Juliana Children's Hospital, Den Haag, the Netherlands,
  Fred Ernst edited by TI

70
- (Concept visual) City of the Netherlands,
  Netherlands Architecture Institute, Rotterdam,
  the Netherlands, TI

72–73
- Photo of Louis Bär
- Harry potter, Istock, stockfoto ID: 458526315
- Summer exhibition 'Powers of Ten', Science Centre NEMO, FP
- Wax figure of Katniss Everdeen, Getty Images,
  stockfoto ID: 460639010
- Stockfoto from istock, logoboom, stockfoto ID: 152949893
- Prehistoric wax figure, Gallo Roman Museum,
  Tongeren, Belgium, EB

74
- Images from the internet, authors unknown

75
- The diagram is based on the ideas of James Campbell and
  the diagram of Christopher Vogler in A Practical Guide to
  Joseph Cambell's The Hero with a Thousand Faces, TI

77
- Concept visual for the Climate House, Oslo, Norway, TI

78
- Nest, Vevey, Switzerland, MB

79
- The American Indian, The New Church,
  Amsterdam, the Netherlands, MB

80
- Dom Under, Domplein Initiative, Utrecht, the Netherlands, MB

81
- Tirpitz, Blåvand, Denmark, EB

82
- Tirpitz, Blåvand, Denmark, MB

83
- Nest, Vevey, Switzerland, MB

84
- Mondriaanhouse, Amersfoort, the Netherlands, MB

85
- Making Peace Festival, Peace Treaty of Utrecht, 2013, TI

86–87
- Concept visual for the National Geographic Campus, Washington D.C., USA, TI

90
- Heineken Experience, Amsterdam, the Netherlands, MB

92
- Book cover of *The Experience Economy Work is Theatre and Every Business a Stage* by Joseph Pine II and James H. Gilmore. Harvard Business Review Press, 1999

94
- Loevestein Castle, Poederoijen, the Netherlands, MB

95
- Tirpitz, Blåvand, Denmark, MB
- World of Silver, Dutch Silver Museum Schoonhoven, the Netherlands, MB

96
- South Holland Heritage House, Heritage South-Holland, Alphen aan de Rijn, MB
- TU Delft Science Centre, the Netherlands, MB

97
- The Story of the Dutch East Indies, Museum Bronbeek, Arnhem, the Netherlands, MB
- Nest, Vevey, Switzerland, MB

99
- Airfork One, Fred and Friends, photo by ditverzinjeniet.nl

100
- Dom Under, Domplein Initiative, Utrecht, the Netherlands, MB and Oliver Shuh

103
- Concept visual Orbis, TI

106
- White Space Creative expedition, Amsterdam, the Netherlands, FP

108
- Concept visual for the Liberty Museum, Nijmegen, the Netherlands, TI

110
- Book cover of *The Never Ending Quest* by Clare W. Graves, ECLET publishing, 2005

111
- Exhibition 'Money for Later', Money Museum, Utrecht, the Netherlands, TI

112
- Montage from different sources, Geert Groote House, Deventer, the Netherlands, MB

113
- Making Peace Festival, Peace Treaty of Utrecht, 2013, TI

114–115
- ASML Experience centre, ASML Veldhoven, the Netherlands, MB

116–117
- Concept visual for the National Geographic Campus, Washington D.C., USA, TI

120
- Forum Romanum, Rome, Italy, EB

121
- Loevestein Castle, Poederoijen, the Netherlands, MB
- Via Appia, Rome, Italy, EB

122
- Tirpitz, Blåvand, Denmark, EB
- Dom Under, Domplein Initiative, Utrecht, the Netherlands, MB

123
- Vatican Museum, Vatican City, EB
- The American Indian, The New Church, Amsterdam, the Netherlands, EB

124–125
- World of Silver, Dutch Silver Museum Schoonhoven, the Netherlands, MB

126
- Museum Rotterdam '40–'45 now, Rotterdam, the Netherlands, TI and MB

127
- Tirpitz, Blåvand, Denmark, EB

128
- Concept visual Friesland Campina Experience Centre, Wageningen, the Netherlands, TI

129
- Friesland Campina Experience Centre, Wageningen, the Netherlands, MB
- EcoNexis house, Zwolle, the Netherlands, MB

130
- ASML Experience centre, ASML Veldhoven, the Netherlands, MB

131
- Friesland Campina Experience Centre, Wageningen, the Netherlands, MB
- ALD Mobility Experience Centre, ALD automotive, Hoofddorp, the Netherlands, Alexander van Berge

132
- Tirpitz, Blåvand, Denmark, Laurian Ghinitoiu

133
- Tirpitz, Blåvand, Denmark, MB

134
- Tirpitz, Blåvand, Denmark, Colin John Seymour

135–136
- Tirpitz, Blåvand, Denmark, p.135: MB, p.136: MB and EB

137
- Tirpitz, Blåvand, Denmark, top photo by Rasmus Hjortshoj, bottom photo by MB

138
- Movie still from 'Saving Private Ryan', DreamWorks, 1998

139
- Airborne Experience, Airborne Museum Hartenstein, Arnhem, the Netherlands, FP
- Bottom right: Museum Rotterdam '40-'45 now, Rotterdam, the Netherlands, Sanne Donders

140
- Concept visuals for the Van Gogh museum, TI

141
- Mondriaanhouse, Amersfoort, the Netherlands, MB

142–145
- Anatomical Theatre, Rijksmuseum Boerhaave, Leiden, the Netherlands, MB

146
- Oh My God, Museum Hilversum, the Netherlands, MB

147–148
- Geert Groote House, Deventer, the Netherlands, EB and MB

149
- Lustrum of the University of Utrecht, the Netherlands, FP

150
- Design Juliana Children's Hospital, Den Haag, the Netherlands, TI

151
- Juliana Children's Hospital, Den Haag, the Netherlands, Fred Ernst

152
- The New Experience, Foundation the New Experience, Arnhem, the Netherlands, MB

153
- Centre for Overweight Adolescent Children's Healthcare, Maastricht UMC+, the Netherlands, MB

154
- Professor Splash, Rotterdam Maritime Museum, the Netherlands, EB

155
- Fortress Pannerden, Gemeente Lingewaarden, Doornenburg, the Netherlands, MB

156
- Loevestein Castle, Poederoijen, The Netherlands, MB
- The Buffel, Rotterdam Maritime Museum, FP
- Fortress Pannerden, Gemeente Lingewaarden, Doornenburg, the Netherlands, Duncan de Fey
- Fortress Pannerden, Gemeente Lingewaarden, Doornenburg, the Netherlands, MB

157
- ICER, Gemeente Oude IJsselstreek, the Netherlands, Fred Ernst
- TU Delft Science Centre, the Netherlands, MB

158–159
- The American Indian, The New Church, Amsterdam, the Netherlands, MB

160
- Designs and photos from The Story of the Dutch East Indies, Museum Bronbeek, Arnhem, the Netherlands, MB, EB and TI

161
- Liberation Route Europe, MB

162–163
- Nest, Vevey, Switzerland, p.162 MB, p.163 EB

164
- Nest, Vevey, Switzerland, EB
- The Story of the Dutch East Indies, Museum Bronbeek, Arnhem, the Netherlands, MB
- Nest, Vevey, Switzerland, MB

165
- The Sea Voyage, National Maritime Museum, Amsterdam, the Netherlands, MB
- Mondriaanhouse, Amersfoort, the Netherlands, MB

166–167
- Anatomical Theatre, Rijksmuseum Boerhaave, Leiden, the Netherlands, MB

168–171
- TU Delft Science Centre, the Netherlands, MB

172–173
- Concept image Artis Museum, TI

174–175
- World of Silver, Dutch Silver Museum Schoonhoven, the Netherlands, MB

176
- Nest, Vevey, Switzerland, EB

177
- Nest, Vevey, Switzerland, Michael Bovay

COLOPHON

Text by Erik Bär and Stan Boshouwers
Cover and visual design by Léon Wijnhoud
Graphic design by Anna Hoving
Diagram design by Britte Hietkamp
Management by Roos Harms and Ingrid Van Ulden
English translations by Mark Hannay, The Language Lab

And a big thanks to the entire Tinker team
for their support and creativity!

www.tinker.nl

BIS Publishers
Building Het Sieraad
Postjesweg 1
1057 DT Amsterdam
the Netherlands
T +31 (0)20 515 02 30
bis@bispublishers.com
www.bispublishers.com

ISBN 978 90 6369 464 7

"We have always tried to be guided by the basic idea that, in the discovery of knowledge, there is great entertainment - as, conversely, in all good entertainment, there is always some grain of wisdom, humanity or enlightenment to be gained."

– Walt Disney –